AMERICAN ALBATROSS

A Twentieth Century Fund Paper

AMERICAN ALBATROSS

THE FOREIGN DEBT DILEMMA

BY ROBERT D. HORMATS

PP Priority Press Publications/New York/1988

The Twentieth Century Fund is a research foundation undertaking timely analyses of economic, political, and social issues. Not-for-profit and nonpartisan, the Fund was founded in 1919 and endowed by Edward A. Filene.

Library of Congress Cataloging-in-Publication Data
Hormats, Robert D.
American albatross: the foreign debt dilemma.

"A Twentieth Century Fund paper"
Includes index.
1. Debts, External—United States. 2. United States —Economic conditions—1981- . 3. United States—Economic policy—1981- . I. Title
HJ8119.H66 1988 336.3'4'0973 88-31816
ISBN 0-87078-220-7
ISBN 0-87078-221-5 (pbk.)

Manufactured in the United States of America.

Foreword

With the rhetoric of the campaign behind them, George Bush and the newly elected Congress must confront the inconsistencies and weaknesses of the nation's economic policies. If they do not quickly gain control over events, events are likely to gain control over them. The job before them is to see to it that the budget deficit is reduced, a credible fiscal policy developed, a fragile financial system shored up, and the current account deficit dealt with.

The informed public is well aware of the dangers of the budget deficit—the creation of the National Economic Commission is a measure of that awareness—and suspects that neither Congress's nor President-elect Bush's commitments to defense, other spending, and taxation add up. The plight of the financial system has been brought home several times, most recently by the shaky condition of the savings and loan system. But few recognize that the current account deficit and America's emergence as the world's largest debtor severely undermine all our efforts to meet our social and economic objectives as well as our capacity to conduct an effective foreign policy.

Robert Hormats, vice-chairman of Goldman, Sachs International Corporation and former assistant secretary of state for economic and business affairs, examines the dangers facing the United States in this paper, one of a series of examinations of the international debt crisis sponsored by the Twentieth Century Fund. He argues persuasively in the following pages that the issue is not whether the U.S. current account deficit will decline substantially—no country can run current account deficits of the magnitude of those now being realized by the United States for very long—but rather how the decline will come about. He warns that the danger is that it will take place in an environment of currency volatility, protectionism, political acrimony, low growth, and high inflation.

To prevent that, Hormats proposes a combination of policies—the pursuit of mutually consistent domestic economic adjustment policies by the United States and its major trading partners, additional moderate changes in exchange rates, reduced constraints on Latin American growth, increased U.S. industrial capacity and productivity, and the maintenance and improvement of a liberal international trade and investment system—that will allow the decline to go on in an orderly, market-oriented manner. His agenda bears heeding at both ends of Pennsylvania Avenue.

Marcia Bystryn, ACTING DIRECTOR
The Twentieth Century Fund
November 1988

Contents

To my parents,
Ruth and Saul Hormats

Introduction

In the course of just four years, from 1983 to 1986, the United States underwent a dramatic transformation—from the world's largest creditor to its largest debtor. The speed with which America's external debt has accumulated and continues to grow threatens to erode this country's ability to attain important domestic economic and social objectives and will jeopardize its capacity to conduct an effective foreign policy for years to come. Increasing external debt, and the extraordinary dependence on imported capital this entails, subjects the U.S. government and American industries, farms, and financial institutions to the perturbations of volatile currency and capital markets; and it imposes larger—and until now unfamiliar—external constraints on many aspects of American national security policy. Virtually every major economic decision by the president, the Congress, and the Federal Reserve Board is likely to be affected by America's large foreign debt. It will be a millstone around the necks of the U.S. government and the private sector for years to come.

In the pages ahead, I shall describe why U.S. external debt has grown so rapidly and what its further accumulation would mean to the American economy and America's position as world leader. I shall also discuss how other nations have coped with large external debt and how American debt differs quantitatively, qualitatively, and in its global impact from that of other countries. And then I will offer a series of recommendations to curb the buildup of U.S. foreign debt in a manner consistent with stable, long-term growth here and abroad. Implementing these recommendations will require changes, not only in American policy but also in our national attitude toward international competition, domestic consumption, and savings. It will necessitate a substantial reallocation of American resources into new productive capacity. And it will call for broader sharing of international responsibility for the health of the world economy and for Western security.

Even as this paper is being completed, in late 1988, U.S. net external debt* is growing rapidly because America's monthly trade deficits, while far lower than in the fall of 1987, are still very large; and interest payments are accelerating on the vast amounts of funds already borrowed from abroad while dividends on direct and equity investment are also rising at a rapid rate. Indeed, in the first quarter of 1988, for the first time in thirty years the United States suffered a net deficit in investment earnings; this led to an increase in this country's current account deficit during a period in which the trade deficit declined. And, it must be recalled, it is the current account deficit, *not* the trade deficit, that must be financed from abroad. U.S. trade deficits and interest payments are likely to remain large for the next several years—leading to a net American debt to the rest of the world approaching $1 trillion early in the next decade.**

---

* In this paper net external debt is defined as the amount by which foreign investment of *all* types in the United States exceeds American investment of *all* types abroad. See Chart 1. It is therefore a shorthand way of describing a country's net internal investment position, and can be used interchangeably with that term. Its components include net direct investment, net equity portfolio investment (common stock), and net financial investment in debt instruments (government and corporate bonds, and bank accounts). It is only the last of these categories that, strictly speaking, should be categorized as "debt." In references to Latin American debt, it is generally figures on financial debt that are cited.

** The size of the current account balance is generally the best guide to change in a country's net international investment position because it measures the net capital flow into or out of a nation. But the net internal investment position is also affected by changes in financial markets and currencies. For example, in 1987 the United States had a current account deficit of $160 billion, but its external debt rose by "only" $99 billion. This reflects the fact that some foreign stock markets rose more than did the U.S. stock market, raising the relative value of U.S. stockholdings abroad; more important, however, was the fact that U.S. assets abroad, denominated in pounds, yen, and deutschemarks rose—when converted back into dollars—quite rapidly because of the rise in these other currencies vis-a-vis the dollar. This helped to keep the net international investment position of America from deteriorating by as much as the current account deficit. For Japan, in 1986 the situation was just the opposite. Its current account surplus was nearly $86 billion while its net external assets rose by only $50 billion, in part because as the yen strengthened, the value of foreign investments in Japan increased quite dramatically when translated back into dollars.

Yet, severe as America's debt problem threatens to become, attempts at "quick-fix" solutions are likely only to cause other problems. It took several years for the United States to build up the large current account deficits that have made it a major debtor, and it will take several years to reduce those deficits. The 1980s will leave the next generation a heavy and painful legacy of debt. It is important to avoid ill-conceived measures predicated on the notion that somehow other nations bear the primary

Chart 1
U.S. International Investment Position
(billion dollars, year end)

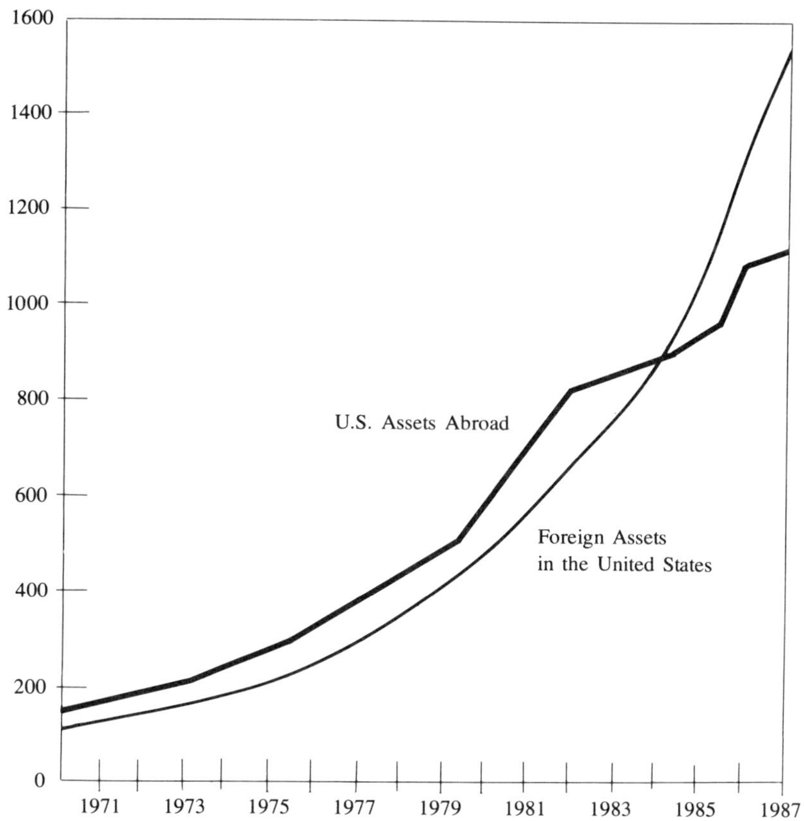

Source: U.S. Department of Commerce, *Survey of Current Business,* June 1987, March 1988; John N. Yochelson, *U.S. Global Economic Strategy: Challenge, Choices, and Priorities* (Washington, D.C.: SIS, September 1988). p. 5.

blame for the problem, or that a rapid reduction in the U.S. current account deficit is possible. Attempts at solutions predicated on such assumptions would compound the debt problem, leading to recession, high inflation, weakened security, fractured alliances, and protectionism.

America's external debt situation differs qualitatively from that of other debtor nations. Because of the great size of the American economy, the key global role of the dollar, and the unique security responsibilities of the United States, this country's external debt has a far more pervasive international impact than the external debt of any other nation. Smaller economies can simply devalue their currencies and expect others to accept their increased exports or reduced imports with relative ease. And if they embark on domestic austerity programs, try to inflate their way out of the problem, reduce military expenditures, or cut foreign aid, it generally has little global impact. This is not the case when the country taking such actions is the United States.

The way in which America's debt buildup is addressed will have a profound effect throughout the world, so its orderly reduction is a matter of considerable interest to other nations, who in turn also have a major interest in facilitating the process. While domestic measures in the United States are critical parts of the answer, collective action by other major countries also is necessary if the accumulation of American debt is to be halted—and ultimately reversed—in a way that does not disrupt growth and price stability in the global economy. Policies to promote higher domestic demand abroad, market-oriented currency adjustments, slower growth of consumption and government spending in the United States, and new investment in plant and equipment in this country are the intelligent alternatives to exchange rate and financial market turbulence, abrupt reductions in American imports induced artificially through protectionism or recession in this country, and disruptive international friction over trade and investment.

The U.S. debt problem forces nations to recognize that we are in the midst of the second great transition of international economic power in this century. After World War I, the United States failed to appreciate the political and economic strength it had inherited from Britain and the responsibility that that strength conferred. It chose to protect its home market rather than champion open trade and did not assist its friends in Europe and Asia to resist aggression until it was almost too late. The world lurched from one trade and financial crisis to another and then to war.

The current transition—from clear American economic preeminence to a broader distribution of international economic strength among the

United States, Europe, Japan, and a number of fast-growing Third World nations—needs to be managed more effectively. The United States remains the nation possessing the greatest combination of economic, political, and military power in the world; it must therefore remain the major factor in maintaining and strengthening a sound economic order. But it cannot do so alone. Other major economies must attach greater priority to reducing or averting large trade imbalances as well as to sustaining world growth. The rules of global competition need to be updated and broadened to include services, agriculture, intellectual property, and investment. Wide gaps in national regulatory practices that distort capital or add to risks in capital markets must be narrowed. And the broader distribution of global economic power must be harnessed to foster a broader sharing of responsibility for Western political stability, security, and support for economic progress in the Third World.

If Americans believe that their allies—who have gained considerable economic strength in recent years—are doing too little to help the United States cut its trade deficit, are moving too slowly to reduce trade barriers, and are not assuming a fair portion of global security responsibilities, then domestic pressures in this nation for trade restrictions, troop withdrawals, and cuts in foreign aid will intensify. At the same time, if America's allies believe they are being unfairly blamed for economic problems largely of this country's own making, if they are pushed to adopt policies counter to their interests, and if U.S. deficits are used as a pretext for our refusing to honor international security, trade, and aid obligations, then these allies might increasingly resist Washington's policy initiatives, and American leadership influence is likely to diminish. Finding common ground and strategies to avoid such friction will be an imperative for national leaders in the years ahead.

The Size and Source of the Debt

At the end of 1987, net U.S. external debt amounted to nearly $370 billion—roughly 8 percent of the U.S. gross national product (GNP). That figure in itself is not alarming, nor are the servicing costs—which come to about one-half of one percent of this nation's GNP. What is alarming is the likelihood that this debt will continue to grow rapidly. In 1988, for example, it will probably increase by about $140 billion—or just over 3 percent of GNP—and virtually every economic forecast projects annual rises of well over $100 billion for the next several years.

This buildup involves a continuation of America's enormous dependence on foreign capital, which in turn creates serious vulnerabilities. If the holders of dollar bonds were to sell them abruptly, or if new capital inflows suddenly dried up, then domestic interest rates would rise sharply as American borrowers were forced to pay more for scarcer capital. The rise in interest rates would significantly slow economic growth. The dollar could collapse, causing havoc in world financial and goods markets and triggering new inflationary pressures in the United States.

But the very effort to maintain the necessary supply of foreign funds to U.S. credit markets carries with it a probability that U.S. interest rates will need to increase to levels that will be high relative to the U.S. domestic rate of inflation in order to ensure that U.S. debt securities remain attractive to foreign citizens. A large external debt, along with a large payments deficit, therefore severely complicates the task of the U.S. government in balancing the key international role of the dollar (as the world's largest reserve and transaction currency) with its role as the domestic currency of the United States. And the dollar's preeminent role in world trade and finance is likely to be tarnished if the currency continues to be volatile and suspect in the eyes of investors.

High levels of external debt also have serious implications for America's leadership of the free world and for its ability to pursue its global security interests. The free world's leader is now its largest debtor. At the same time, nations without a tradition of postwar political or alliance leadership now are the world's major creditors. This situation represents a *terra incognita*. It raises questions that go far beyond economics. Can the United States retain its international leadership role if it piles up large external debts year after year? Can U.S. domestic political support for foreign aid, liberal trade, and a credible American military presence overseas be sustained in this high-debt, large trade deficit environment? Can the political-economic order created in the immediate post–World War II period, when the United States enjoyed a remarkable margin of resources and economic power relative to all other nations, hold together as U.S. economic strength, on which that order has depended, declines relative to other nations? Can the United States successfully lead alliances in which tensions over trade, payments imbalances, and military burden sharing increase? Will other countries in these alliances devote substantial amounts of financial resources to serving Western political or security goals if the United States reduces foreign troop levels, foreign aid, and other forms of support?

But just as the high level of American foreign debt raises problems, so will the painful process of reducing it. Few of America's trading partners are eager to accept the large reductions in their surpluses with the

United States, which are the counterpart to the needed decline in the U.S. trade deficit. To eliminate the U.S. trade deficit would require America's trading partners to relinquish collectively $170 billion in net exports. Most will face stiff resistance from affected sectors at home to the decline in exports and increases in imports that must inevitably be involved in this process.

Economic history will record the 1970s as the Decade of Inflation and the 1980s as the Decade of Debt: enormous Third World debt as well as massive U.S. government, corporate, consumer, and foreign debt. Because debt is a seamless web, it must be reduced carefully. Attempting to abruptly halt the accumulation of U.S. foreign debt by sharply reducing internal growth risks default on outstanding domestic debt in the highly leveraged American economy and a deterioration in the precarious Third World debt situation. Too quick a dollar decline—while not without benefits for much of American industry—risks unleashing domestic inflation, pushing up domestic interest rates, and creating recession in America's major trading partners. A resort to protectionism in this country would have similar negative effects.

In the final analysis, no country can run current account deficits of the magnitude of those now being realized by the United States for very long. The question is not whether the U.S. current account deficit will decline substantially. It must, because foreign investors and central banks will not finance such deficits indefinitely. The question is how that decline will occur. That can happen as the result of an orderly, market-oriented process involving a combination of increases in U.S. productive capacity, exchange rate adjustments, faster growth in demand in America's trading partners, cuts in the growth of America's consumption and in the country's budget deficit, higher U.S. savings and manufacturing investment, and an improvement in the Third World debt situation; or it can occur in a disorderly way, in an environment of currency volatility, protectionism, political acrimony, low growth, and high inflation. Finding the right combination of policies to correct these imbalances in an orderly fashion is one of the major global economic and political challenges of the next few years.

1 / Debt—Early American Style

It started in New York in 1817. English bankers and merchants, eager to invest in the fast-developing American economy, purchased bonds issued by New York State to finance the construction of the Erie Canal. Impressed by New York's successful sale of these bonds, other states began to borrow in London to finance the construction of railways, canals, harbors, and toll roads. Private banks in the South also borrowed heavily to finance the boom in cotton production. Between 1820 and 1840, the total debt of the American states rose dramatically from $13 million to $200 million—the "greater part . . . in foreign portfolios."[1]

But this boom in foreign lending did not proceed smoothly. Many banks failed in the Panic of 1837,* which was brought on by a collapse in real estate and commodity prices as a result of the inability of a number of banks to repay their notes, as promised, in the form of gold or silver. When that happened American financial stability became suspect, and in rapid succession the country's credit suffered abroad, foreign capital inflows virtually ceased, and a serious depression began. In the early 1840s the economy's poor performance—the depression lasted a full five years—led to a dramatic loss of state revenues, bond defaults, and, ultimately, repudiation of state obligations. By 1842 the credit of the United States was so poor that the federal Treasury itself was unable to borrow money in London.

America's fortunes improved later in the 1840s. The railway-building boom—triggered by James Marshall's discovery in 1848 at Sutter's Mill and the subsequent California gold rush, increasing cotton prices, and stronger agricultural production— stimulated investment and attracted new capital flows to the United States. The states again began to service their debts, and once more the funds came—mostly from England. But this time the large borrowers included private railway companies. By

* Financial crises in those days were called "panics" because they tended to be associated with panic withdrawals from banks and panic selling of stocks and commodities.

1857 American foreign indebtedness reached roughly $1.3 billion, and fully one-quarter ($500 million) of U.S. corporate securities were owned by foreigners.[2] This influx of foreign capital enabled the United States to finance its trade and current account deficits. From 1851 to 1860, imports averaged $284 million annually; exports averaged $250 million. As demand grew for imported steel to build new railways, capital equipment for new factories, and farm tools to work new lands, the flows of foreign financing accelerated.

Unfortunately, recovery proved short-lived. In the Panic of 1857, the failure of the Ohio Life Insurance and Trust Company touched off a financial collapse, caused in part by speculation in railroad securities and real estate.[3] A flow of American gold to Europe as a result of the negative trade balance exacerbated the problem. Stock market and commodity prices collapsed, contributing to a banking crisis. British bankers called in loans, thus precipitating a rise in American interest rates, which further weakened the economy. Another depression followed.

Fueled in part by large government deficits, the economy soon recovered. The Civil War led to massive increases in federal borrowing—with public debt in 1865 reaching a record $2.8 billion—and to substantial further capital flows from abroad to finance weapons and equipment. During this period, American companies became increasingly dependent on funds from Europe, both to finance new investment—particularly in railroads—and to help refinance existing debt. The U.S. trade balance, which had recorded a $110 million surplus in 1860, fell to a deficit in 1865 and remained weak. The Panic of 1873—triggered by railroad speculation combined with overexpansion in industry, agriculture, and commerce—led to yet another depression. And that depression was made worse by a contraction in foreign demand for American commodity exports because of recession in Europe and by a dramatic liquidity squeeze on American companies due to a curtailment of the flow of funds from England.

Defaults again took place. At the end of 1874, roughly 40 percent of the foreign-owned railway bonds were not paying interest. Many of these bonds were again serviced after a time, and, when they were, their rate of return was roughly double that which investors received on bonds issued by English companies.[4] European borrowers had demanded and received a high risk premium for their loans to Americans. Over time that led to a good return for many of them, even though less-fortunate investors suffered sizable losses.

The U.S. depression also brought an improvement in America's balance of payments. Imports declined sharply while foreign demand for U.S.

commodity exports gained strength as Europe recovered more quickly than America. By 1874 the United States had a trade surplus—its first since the Civil War; by 1877 it had its first current account surplus since the Civil War. These improvements slowed the buildup of U.S. external debt and helped the United States regain its creditworthiness.

The road again turned rocky in the 1890s. Imports grew rapidly as the economy boomed. The U.S. government, as it had in 1816, 1824, and 1828, raised tariffs sharply. Protection combined with financial excesses in the United States and in Europe led to the Panic of 1893, which saw a major stock market crash and a sharp fall in U.S. gold stocks. The panic had its origins in the failure of the British banking house of Baring Brothers; that led British investors to sell British as well as American securities. At the time, the United States had a net external debt of roughly 25 percent of GNP. Sales of U.S. securities brought about a drain in gold from the United States—and higher U.S. interest rates. Once more, there were bank and railway failures in this country, and yet another depression. Before 1893 had ended, "491 banks and over 15,000 businesses were reputed to have failed. Before the turning point was reached in 1897, about one-third of the total railroad mileage was in the hands of receivers."[5]

In the late 1890s, a series of railroad, utility, and industrial consolidations took place. Exports of agricultural and manufactured goods boomed, and the American economy prospered. In the last two years of the nineteenth century, the U.S. trade surplus exceeded $500 million. In 1900 U.S. imports totaled $929 million, while exports reached $1.5 billion. Substantial amounts of new investment were attracted from Britain, Holland, and other parts of Europe.

While the young and predominantly agricultural American economy of the nineteenth century differed dramatically from the highly industrialized, high-technology economy of the late twentieth century, this brief account highlights two points that are still relevant. First, large U.S. external borrowing and foreign debt were not a serious *long-term* problem one hundred years ago, because most of the borrowed funds were used for productive investment. The imported capital helped to build new plants and finance new equipment as well as to construct a massive infrastructure of highways, waterworks, and railroads. U.S. investment abroad remained small because Americans were using their growing wealth to make profitable investments at home. The U.S. external debt was manageable because the productive capacity it helped to finance enabled Americans to generate a high volume of manufactured and agricultural exports that earned funds to service and repay the borrowed money. In sharp contrast, a large portion of the funds borrowed from abroad in recent years has been used directly or indirectly to finance the growth of the U.S. budget deficit and private consumption. This use of funds raises valid concerns about the ability of the United States to service, and work down, its debt without imposing enormous strain on existing capacity.

Second, even though most of the funds borrowed abroad in the nineteenth century were used for productive purposes, dependence on foreign capital still carried serious risks. As noted, foreign investors withheld new money when they perceived a weakening of U.S. creditworthiness or when economic difficulties in their home countries led to a drying up of funds for investment. When these capital flows slowed or stopped, there was a severe liquidity squeeze in the United States: interest rates rose and growth fell. This sequence of events in turn increased the severity of the panics. A similar type of squeeze would take place today if foreign investors withheld loans to the United States, or demanded a considerably higher risk premium to compensate for higher inflation or an expected decline in the dollar. In the nineteenth century the weakening in the U.S. economy resulting from liquidity squeezes helped to reduce America's trade and current account deficits but caused severe dislocations of labor and manufacturing in the process, including frequent bankruptcies. That could happen again.

In the beginning of the twentieth century, Americans began to use funds earned from their booming raw material and industrial exports to invest abroad. U.S. direct investment abroad rose from $634 million in 1897 to $2.6 billion in 1914. This helped the United States to assume the status of net international creditor. And huge sums—roughly $9 billion—were lent to the Allies to support their mobilization in World War I. After that war Americans extended large loans to Europe, and significant U.S. direct investment took place there as Americans actively financed the reconstruction effort. In 1919 total U.S. foreign direct investment amounted to $3.8 billion, and its trade surplus to $3.3 billion. American investments overseas began to earn substantial dividends and interest, ultimately offsetting the large earnings foreigners were continuing to enjoy from investments made earlier in the United States.

In the aftermath of World War II, American government loans to Europe, plus continued corporate investment there, added to America's positive net international investment position. By 1946 America's net creditor position came to $4.1 billion; it rose to $15 billion in 1948 and then to $24.3 billion in 1958—by which time U.S. overseas direct investments reached $27 billion. Today, as a legacy of this period, the United States still earns large dividends on its direct investments overseas.

2 / How the United States Accumulated Its Large Debt

Through World War II and for the twenty-five years that followed, the United States realized merchandise trade surpluses every year. In all but three years between 1946 and 1970, these trade surpluses, added to earnings on direct investments abroad, easily offset the large amounts of capital the United States was exporting to the rest of the world in the form of foreign aid, security assistance, and overseas military expenditures. During this period the United States accumulated substantial foreign assets. By 1970 these assets were valued at more than $165 billion, roughly half in the form of direct investment, while foreign assets in the United States came to just under $107 billion. As a result the net creditor position of the United States in 1970 was close to $60 billion.

In 1971 America's trade balance slipped from a surplus to a deficit of just over $4 billion. But despite a weakening American trade position over the next nine years (in 1980 the U.S. trade deficit was $31 billion), the country ran a slight current account surplus. American earnings on international business services (airfares, insurance and banking, lawyers' fees, and payment for use of licenses) plus income from direct investments abroad more than offset the trade deficits. America's net creditor position grew to $106 billion by 1980. Current account surpluses enabled Americans to purchase more assets abroad than foreigners purchased in the United States. In 1981 America's creditor position reached its high-water mark—over $140 billion.[1]

In 1982, though, the growing trade deficit began to swamp surpluses on business services and investment income. The current account fell to an $8 billion deficit. This was the beginning of a relentless deterioration of the U.S. current account—to a deficit of $116 billion in 1985 and nearly $140 billion in 1986—and consequently of a shift of the United States from the world's largest creditor to its largest debtor. At the end of 1985, net U.S. external debt reached nearly $111 billion: by the end of 1986 it had grown to roughly $270, and by the end of 1987 it had risen to over $368 billion.

The term "debt" is used loosely here. The primary change between 1982 and 1986 was the reversal in the U.S. net international investment position; that is, total foreign investment in the United States (in corporate equities, plants, real estate, and financial debt instruments) overtook total U.S. investment of a similar nature abroad. If debt were taken to mean only "financial debt," for example, notes and bonds, the United States became a net debtor in 1971—the year foreigners came to hold more financial debt instruments in the United States than Americans held abroad. But in 1971 American direct investment abroad so greatly exceeded foreign direct investment in the United States that the difference made up for the negative U.S. balance with respect to financial debt instruments. For a long time, foreigners have held more U.S. corporate equities than Americans held foreign equities, but this also was outweighed by the strong U.S. direct investment position abroad. Thus the term "net debtor" as used here means that the United States has a net deficit on *overall* international investment; that is, foreign citizens have more investment in U.S. assets than Americans have abroad.

The question we now turn to is how the United States got into this position—and why this imbalance has grown so rapidly.

The U.S. debt problem of the 1980s has its roots in the Great Inflation of the 1970s. During that turbulent decade, inflation increased dramatically in virtually every industrialized and developing nation, causing a sharp drop in purchasing power, extremely high interest rates, and poor growth performance. The twin oil shocks—the first following the 1973 Yom Kippur War and the second following the fall of the shah of Iran—were major contributors to the inflationary surge. But there were also important domestic causes. These included the sizable increases in government spending and lax monetary policy in most industrialized countries. From 1946 to 1967 the U.S. federal deficit grew at an annual rate averaging less than 0.2 percent; from 1968 to 1980, U.S. federal deficits rose to an annual growth rate of 2 percent. The growth of annual deficits in Britain, France, West Germany, and Japan collectively rose from 0.7 percent before 1968 to over 2 percent from 1968 to 1988. Significant increases in the money supply in the United States—where M-1 (the most frequently cited monetary aggregate) rose from an average 2.5 percent per year from 1947 to 1967 to 6.4 percent from 1968 to 1980—and to a lesser degree in other major Western economies led to a sharp drop in real interest rates.

With stocks and bonds rendered increasingly unattractive to many investors by low real interest rates, upward pressure on prices, and high inflationary expectations, a large portion of the liquidity in the system went into investment in hard items, the prices of which skyrocketed. Large-scale industrial stockpiling of commodities and other goods, easily financed and a good hedge against further price increases, also contributed to inflationary pressures. A number of the largest developing countries, particularly in Latin America, borrowed heavily based on the assumption that prices for their raw materials and manufactured exports would continue to rise for the foreseeable future, enabling them to service and repay their debts with relative ease. U.S. and foreign commercial banks—looking for outlets to re-lend petrodollar deposits—made big loans based on a similar calculation.

For a time, businesses in many sectors (for example, steel, chemicals, energy, agriculture, autos) added substantial new capacity around the world in the belief that price increases would continue and that new investment, financed with low-cost money, would earn a high return; debts, in turn, could be repaid with inflated currency. A recently published analysis of the European chemical industry describes "a massive excess of capacity for bulk products, which reflected both inflated extrapolations of demand growth from the late 1970s and overinvestment not only by existing producers, who borrowed heavily to finance this, but also by the major oil companies."[2] There was relatively little concentration on industrial efficiency because inefficient practices could readily be passed on to buyers in the form of higher prices. And governments could borrow large sums knowing that their debts would be paid off in cheaper money.

By the end of the 1970s, however, this set of circumstances had wreaked havoc on virtually all economies. Inflation had seriously eroded wealth, raised raw material and labor costs, and pushed nominal interest rates to astronomical heights, thus deterring large, new investments and causing high unemployment in the United States and throughout the world. Americans were demanding, with increasing intensity, that their leaders curb the high rate of inflation and attack the policies that fed it. Inflation became a central issue in the 1980 presidential election. Similar frustrations influenced elections abroad. In virtually every large Western nation in the early 1980s, the leader, or governing party, was voted out of office in favor of those who the public believed could more effectively confront pressing economic problems, particularly the scourge of rising prices and diminishing real incomes.

Bolstered by strong anti-inflation mandates, most of those new leaders set about to curb government budget deficits and cut spending, and central banks in virtually all countries moved vigorously to tighten domestic credit. Together these policies—which mutually reinforced one another across borders—led to the deepest recession in the industrialized world since World War II. But they also broke the back of inflation.

Europe experienced a severe and prolonged recession as its leaders steadfastly held to their goal of cutting budgets while monetary policy was severely restrained. Margaret Thatcher in Britain, Helmut Kohl in West Germany, and Ruud Lubbers in the Netherlands recognized that only an end to inflation and inflationary expectations would restore confidence among investors and establish a basis for sound future growth. The new Mitterrand government in France, after flirting with expansionary budgets, became convinced that it could not run large budget deficits without a serious deterioration in its balance of payments while West Germany and its other neighbors were pursuing tight money-tight spending policies.

Collectively, these policies curtailed demand, and in turn investment, while gross savings grew. Europe became a sluggish market for imports and for its own production while weak private and government demand for capital made that continent an important exporter of funds. Declining growth in Europe encouraged its industries to look abroad for markets; when the U.S. economy picked up in 1983, those industries were ready and able to sell here.

In Japan the situation was much the same. To counter inflation Tokyo cut spending, and the Bank of Japan restrained credit. Domestic demand slowed dramatically, industries intensified their export efforts, and additional capital was available for investment abroad. The most attractive destination for both goods and capital was the United States.

Policies of the United States differed considerably from those abroad. (See Chart 2.) Both President Ronald Reagan and the Federal Reserve Board repeatedly emphasized their commitment to fight inflation, but the president had other items on his agenda as well. His overriding goal was to reduce the role of government in the U.S. economy and society; he believed that by cutting taxes, thereby depriving Congress of money to spend, he could shrink the many domestic programs he considered too intrusive and too costly. Some of his economic advisers also argued that a major tax cut would free up private funds for new investment and trigger a surge in American growth; that in turn would generate sufficient revenue to miraculously shrink the budget deficit, even in the face of the big tax cut and the large increases in military appropriations which the president insisted on to boost America's defense capability.

The Reagan program received strong support from Congress and the public based on the widespread belief that the country was overtaxed, social programs had expanded too rapidly, the military had been underfunded, and investment needed a shot in the arm. Few argued that the magnitude of the tax cut and the increase in military expenditures were too large; and those who did received little attention.

Although America's trading partners may have doubted the wisdom of the big budget deficits the U.S. was accruing, they were in deep reces-

Chart 2
Divergent Fiscal Policies: 1981–84
(percentage of GNP)

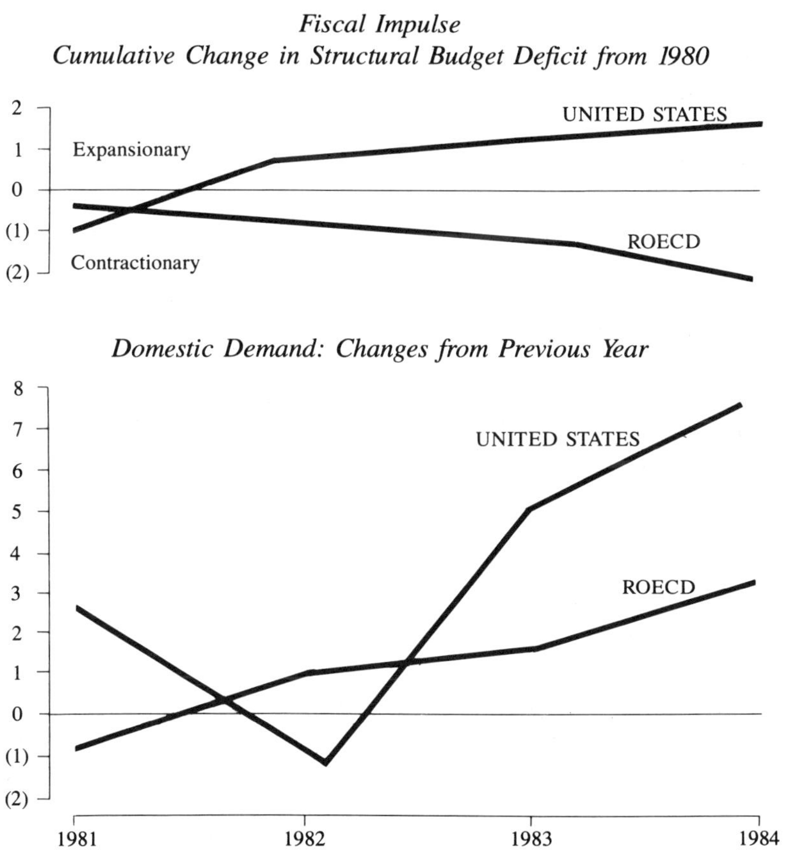

Source: OECD Economic Outlook, no. 35, June 1984.
ROECD = The rest of the OECD area (the figures in the top panel are for the six largest OECD countries other than the United States).

sion and soon found the stimulus these policies provided to U.S. growth, and hence to their exports, to be attractive. Although critics abroad said that the United States was absorbing too much foreign capital, investment opportunities in much of the rest of the world were relatively limited at the time. A large portion of the capital that flowed to the United States during the early 1980s probably would have earned a lower return at home.

Because U.S. fiscal policy was not being employed in the fight against inflation (although deregulation and a tough line on the air traffic controller's strike were used as anti-inflation weapons), the Federal Reserve had to bear the primary burden for that fight. It did so with the only instrument it had at its disposal—monetary policy. In 1979 it sharply raised the discount rate and tightened credit, which caused U.S. interest rates to rise to levels much higher than in other large Western nations. Dollar securities then became highly attractive to foreign investors. Many of them had a relatively low portion of dollar assets in their portfolios in contrast to assets denominated in other currencies. Foreign demand for dollars with which to purchase American assets increased; the dollar surged. To stop the decline in their currencies (which they feared would rekindle inflationary pressures), Japan, West Germany, and other major trading nations raised interest rates—thus retarding their economic recovery. Companies in those countries, facing a weak market at home and finding themselves more competitive in the American market because of the strong dollar, increased sales to the United States.

But interest rate differentials between the United States and other major economies cannot account completely for the dollar's sharp ascent in 1984 and 1985. The big interest rate differential in favor of dollar assets had passed by 1983, and U.S. interest rates also fell sharply during most of 1984, when the dollar continued to appreciate. (See Chart 3.) A major reason for the the dollar's steady rise during this period was the complex interaction between a rising budget deficit on the one hand and an improving inflationary performance (and confidence in the Federal Reserve's continuing commitment to fight inflation) on the other; this led to a boom in the bond market and confidence in the dollar.

Growing federal budget deficits generated a high rate of growth—domestic demand grew at a rate of 7.5 percent in 1983 and 1984—and in turn massive demand for capital, which could not be met from domestic savings, but rapidly rising budget deficits normally tend to destroy confidence in a country's currency rather than strengthen it. In the United States, however, other circumstances worked in the opposite direction.

Dramatic progress was being made in fighting inflation. The collapse in oil prices helped, as did the high dollar because it caused a large portion of the surge in domestic spending (which might otherwise have generated domestic inflationary pressures and caused the Federal Reserve to tighten monetary policy) to go to imports. Import prices fell due to intense foreign competition for the U.S. market and overcapacity abroad. That held down U.S. prices and wages. The Federal Reserve, as a result of declining prices, could progressively lower interest rates to boost growth. Lower inflation, and a Federal Reserve policy of cutting interest rates while retaining its credibility as a resolute inflation fighter, helped to generate a rise in bond prices.

Chart 3
Interest Rates and the Exchange Rate

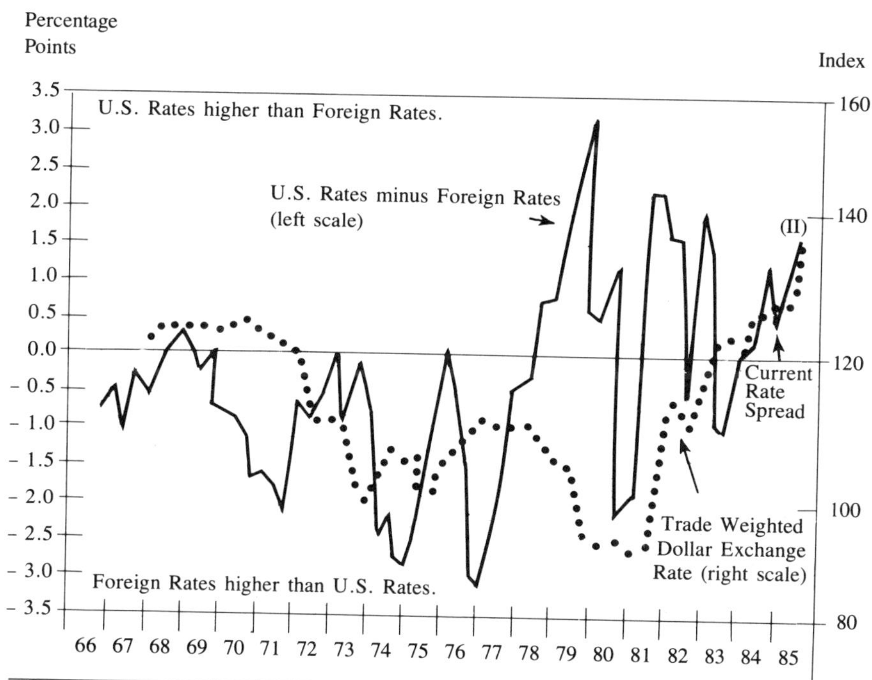

Sources: Federal Reserve Board, Organization for Economic Cooperation and Development, Morgan Guaranty Trust Co.

U.S. Rate: three-month Treasury bill rate.

Foreign Interest Rates: Average equivalent short-term money-market rates of ten industrial countries weighted by their share of U.S. trade from 1972 to 1976.

For a time, these circumstances induced foreign investors, notwithstanding the growing budget and trade deficits, to place enormous sums in the U.S. bond market, in the process helping to finance the U.S. budget deficit and driving the dollar further up (also a source of profit to these investors), thereby further reducing inflationary pressures. In 1982 foreign private investors bought $4 billion of U.S. corporate and Treasury bonds combined. In 1983 that figure reached over $15 billion. In 1984 it shot up to $33 billion; and in 1985, to over $60 billion.

Boosted by fiscal stimulus and declining interest rates, the United States became the first major economy to emerge vigorously from recession—growing faster than its trading partners, absorbing more imports, and borrowing large sums of money to finance government and private credit needs. Until 1986 foreign private investors remained willing to buy large quantities of dollar-denominated debt instruments, thus permitting the United States to finance its large and growing trade and budget deficits with relative ease. Its financial markets, particularly its bond market, continued to be attractive, the inflation climate was good, and business profitability appeared strong.

In short, the inflation in the 1970s, and the dramatic difference between America's efforts to counter it and those of its major trading partners, set the stage for the debt problems of the 1980s. The U.S. policy mix—using tight money to fight inflation while the budget deficit was growing—differed radically from that of its trading partners, who pursued more prudent fiscal as well as monetary policies. These policies led to a surge in U.S. borrowing and consumption, heavy reliance on foreign capital, a decline in the price competitiveness of U.S. goods due to the high dollar, and growing imports of foreign-made goods.

Other major trading nations supplied both capital and goods in great abundance. To them the United States was the "market of last resort" and "the borrower of last resort." The competitive developing countries of East Asia also intensified marketing efforts in the growing and relatively open American market. High-debt countries in Latin America, suffering from the downturn in the world economy (which caused a collapse in prices of the commodity exports on which they depend in substantial measure) and from their own excessive and often misused borrowing, cut their imports and increased exports in an effort to stop the accumulation of foreign debt and to obtain more hard currency with which to pay interest on funds already borrowed. The trade surplus that the United States traditionally enjoyed with these countries was quickly reversed.

Developments from 1981 to 1985—A Closer Look

The series of large annual deficit budgets proposed by the president and passed by the Congress when monetary policy was aimed at fighting inflation caused internal and external distortions. Government demand for goods and services increased—particularly in the area of defense, where expenditures rose by 13.5 percent. Tax cuts combined with increased government benefits (for example, entitlements—most indexed to inflation and not "means tested," that is, provided without a test of the need of the recipient—climbed by 9.4 percent) enabled large numbers of Americans to increase consumption—at least temporarily. Increased household borrowing added to consumer demand. In the late 1970s personal spending hovered around 63 percent of GNP. In this period it rose to about 66 percent of GNP. This additional spending, along with the favorable depreciation allowances and investment tax credits contained in the 1981 tax reforms, served to stimulate private-sector investments for a time.

Increased consumer credit, higher private investment, and accelerating public-sector financial demands led to a surge in U.S. borrowing. In 1980 government and private debt stood at 137 percent of GNP, which was roughly in line with the norm of the 1950s, 1960s, and 1970s; by the end of 1985, that debt had grown to an extraordinary 170 percent of GNP. Household debt had increased by 7.6 percent of GNP (from 50.9 percent of GNP to 58.5 percent), business debt by 7.6 percent of GNP (from 50.3 percent of GNP to 57.9 percent), and federal government debt by 13.3 percent of GNP (from 26.1 percent of GNP to 39.4 percent).[3]

There was not enough domestic capital to meet this big increase in borrowing. From 1973 to 1981, the U.S. gross domestic private savings rate equaled roughly 18 percent of GNP. But because gross domestic private investment averaged only 16.7 percent, and the government budget deficit was less than 1 percent of GNP, the nation had a small surplus of savings to invest abroad. By 1985, gross domestic private investment (notwithstanding a big increase in 1984) was at roughly its 1973–81 average (16.8 percent of GNP), and gross domestic savings were at roughly the 1973–81 average; but the government's deficit amounted to 3.5 percent of GNP. Private savings were not adequate to finance that deficit plus private investment requirements. Financing from abroad was required. As the gap between domestic savings and domestic credit needs opened up, the current account deficit jumped spectacularly. From roughly $9 billion in 1982, it grew to $116 billion in 1985, and to $160 billion in 1987.

It is worth repeating that it was the *interaction* between the federal deficit and Federal Reserve policy that permitted the current account deficit to rise. Without foreign capital, the federal deficit would have crowded out private investment, the dollar would not have risen as sharply, and inflation would have been higher But with an improving U.S. anti-inflation performance and market confidence in the outlook for non-inflationary growth, foreign suppliers of capital remained willing to finance the gap between U.S. savings and U.S. credit needs for a surprisingly long period of time.

The tax cuts and increased expenditures that put more money in the pockets of individual consumers helped sectors such as housing, whose products do not compete with foreign imports. But their effect on capital inflow, and the higher dollar, hurt industries that depend heavily on exports or that are sensitive to import competition. The tax cut, and the added government expenditures for defense and entitlements, was paid for, in a very real sense, by U.S. exporters and those industries and workers who had to compete with the surge of imports.

In 1981, U.S. exports were $239 billion; by 1985 they had fallen to $219 billion. During that same period, imports shot up from $273 billion to $352 billion. The deterioration in trade was enormous in certain areas: the surplus in chemicals fell from $11 billion to $7 billion; the deficit in basic manufacturing worsened from $18 billion to $35 billion; the balance in machinery and transportation equipment dropped from a surplus of $25 billion to a deficit of $44 billion; and the balance in food and live animals slipped from a surplus of $14 billion to a deficit of $1 billion. The deterioration took place vis-a-vis most of America's trading partners: The U.S. deficit of $18 billion with Japan in 1981 fell to $50 billion in 1985; the U.S. deficit with Canada slipped from $2 billion in 1981 to $16 billion; U.S. trade with the European Community declined from an $11 billion surplus in 1981 to a $23 billion deficit in 1985; and a $1 billion surplus with Latin America in 1981 became an $18 billion deficit by 1985. The only improvement was vis-a-vis OPEC, where a $30 billion deficit in 1981 shrank to an $11 billion deficit in 1985.

In 1981—the high-water mark for the United States as a creditor nation—aggregate U.S. investment abroad was $720 billion while aggregate foreign investment in the U.S. was $579 billion. In 1985, as the result of the escalation of the U.S. current account deficits, overall American external obligations rose to roughly $1.06 trillion while American investments abroad rose to $950 billion. The United States became a debtor to the world of nearly $111 billion. (See Chart 4.) Breaking down these figures: The amount of aggregate foreign direct investment in the United States increased from $109 billion in 1981 to $185 billion in 1985. The value of foreign portfolio investments in American corporate securities rose from $75 billion to $206 billion. It is important to note here that much of this increase resulted not from foreign purchase of U.S. equities during this period, which averaged less than

Chart 4
U.S. Current Account and Net Assets, 1970–87

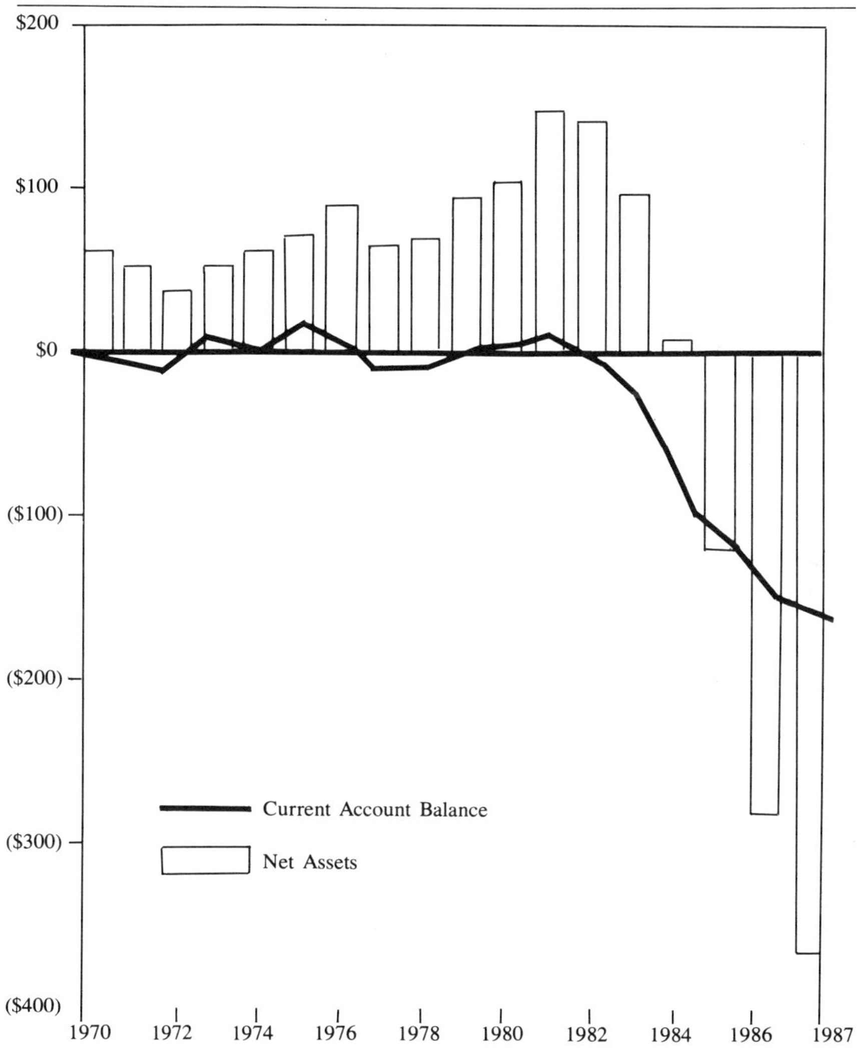

Source: U.S. Department of Commerce, *Survey of Current Business.*

$5 billion per year, but from the rise in foreign holdings of U.S. financial debt instruments (bonds). The rising bond market boosted the value of foreign assets in this category, but the more striking factor was the inflow of new funds; net foreign purchase of corporate debt alone amounted to over $60 billion in the years 1983–85 combined, compared to less than $9 billion in the three previous years combined.

The buildup of American obligations in this last category poses a number of problems. In the five-year period 1981–85, U.S. gross financial debt rose from 13 percent of GNP to 19 percent, and from 103 percent of U.S. exports to 210 percent of U.S. exports. Interest payments on this financial debt rose from 10 percent of exports to 16 percent of exports. As shall be discussed in Chapter 5, this type of asset has enormous potential for *volatility.* Bonds, for example, are far more easily bought and sold than companies (a point to be borne in mind later in reviewing domestic concerns about the surge in foreign direct investment in 1986 and 1987). A collapse in foreign confidence in the American economy could lead to a major shift out of U.S. government and corporate bonds, and U.S. bank deposits, into foreign securities and bank deposits (and perhaps precious metals), causing turmoil in capital and currency markets. Thus the *type* of debt that the United States has been building up—should it continue—is just as alarming as its magnitude.

During this period, foreign companies, helped by the rising dollar, made intense marketing efforts in the United States, and they made new investments at home to produce goods tailored to American needs and tastes.

At the same time, the high dollar discouraged American investment at home in new manufacturing capacity, particularly in the area of capital goods such as machine tools and many types of consumer goods. So not only was the United States accumulating debt, it was also experiencing a reduction of its capacity to service it. As the then Federal Reserve chairman, Paul Volcker, observed, "Individuals, businesses and government have collectively been spending more than we produce. That might be acceptable if we were matching the foreign borrowing with a surge in productive investment in the United States. That has been the case at times in the distant past in the United States and in other countries more recently. But it is consumption that has been leading the economic parade." It is, Volcker stated, "not sustainable from an economic perspective to pile up foreign debts while failing to make the investment that we need both to generate growth and to service the debts."[4]

The economy's continued failure to generate a significant increase in capital investment would mean that much of the growth in U.S. exports—

particularly manufactured exports—needed to reduce the American current account deficit would have to come through a sharp reduction in future domestic consumption; that is, without new productive capacity, far more of what Americans produce would need to be exported, and far less consumed. Domestic consumption would have to slow considerably, or increasing exports would put pressure on industrial capacity and in so doing generate inflationary pressures.

The best way to reduce the rate of growth of consumption without damaging the domestic economy is to cut the budget deficit gradually. But here, too, the early 1980s has left a substantial structural problem. Keynesian economists make the point that during periods of recession a deficit is appropriate because it stimulates growth; but they also argue that government should run surpluses during periods of vigorous growth, when fiscal stimulus is no longer needed. During the administrations of Franklin D. Roosevelt, Harry S. Truman, and Dwight D. Eisenhower, Keynesian deficits were utilized to pull the economy out of recession but were avoided during more normal times. In John F. Kennedy's administration, deficits were justified not only to get the country out of recession, but also to attain full employment; that is, they were utilized when the economy was growing modestly (although not fast enough to achieve full employment) to raise growth to levels that would attain full employment. That broke precedent with traditional U.S. fiscal practice; thereafter, deficits were "accepted" as legitimate even during periods of economic growth, and public attitudes toward them became increasingly lax.

The Reagan deficits were, except in the early years of his administration, even more of a departure from Keynes. They grew dramatically not only during a recession, not only in a period of modest growth, but also during the *high point* of the longest economic recovery in the postwar period—meaning that the U.S. government was accumulating debt rapidly when growth was strong, and it should have been taking in added revenue sufficient to reduce the deficit. Indeed, after six years of recovery the United States should have been able to produce a budget surplus; instead, we are currently running an annual deficit of over $150 billion.

Developments Abroad

A country cannot import capital unless other countries are capable of, and willing to, export it. The ability of other nations to achieve current account surpluses and supply the United States with capital is the result of their surpluses of domestic savings over domestic investment. Foreign credit has permitted the United States to run sustained current account deficits and, domestically, to finance its federal deficit without crowding out private-sector borrowing.

Japan. In the postwar period, the Japanese have maintained a consistently high savings rate. Japan's institutions and attitudes, formed in the late 1940s and 1950s, at a time of economic insecurity and weakness, were geared to generate savings and discourage excessive consumption, thus providing substantial funds for industrial investment. For example, the Japanese save to pay the bulk of home purchases in cash because they cannot deduct mortgage interest from their taxes; they save more for old age because social security programs are limited in scope. Moreover, until recently there have been tax advantages to certain types of savings accounts; for example, interest on the first three million yen in many personal savings accounts was not taxed. In addition, the broad use of the bonus system (that is, providing a large portion of an employee's salary in the form of an end-of-year, lump-sum bonus) tends to favor savings; a recent study found that Japanese regard bonuses as separate from the rest of their income and that roughly 50 percent of bonuses are saved. As a result of these policies, Japanese household savings have traditionally averaged around 20 percent of GNP per year—more than four times that of the United States.[5]

During most of the 1970s, Japan's savings rate was roughly in line with its domestic investment requirements. After 1980, however, the rate of domestic investment fell partly because of weakening domestic demand. During this same period, Tokyo moved to reduce the country's large budget deficit (it was cut from 7.3 percent of GNP in 1981 to 3.6 percent in 1985) in order to reverse the buildup of government debt, which then stood at close to 70 percent of GNP, compared to roughly 50 percent for the United States.

Tokyo's aim in cutting the deficit was to avoid crowding out private borrowing once the economy achieved faster growth. It feared that future government borrowing could force up interest rates, thus weakening prospects for private investment by making potential projects more expensive. There was also a danger that high deficits would contribute to excessive private demand, higher inflation, and a weakened current account position. Consumer price inflation had risen from 2.1 percent in early 1979 to 9.5 percent in early 1980, largely due to the OPEC oil shock, while the current account surplus of $26.5 billion in 1978 had fallen to a $10.7 billion deficit in 1980. In addition, the government took the view that failure to make big spending cuts in the early 1980s would make the country more vulnerable to runaway deficits later, when a rapidly aging population would seek greater social benefits.

The fall in investment and cuts in government spending led to a weakening in domestic demand. They also reduced the domestic need for Japan's abundant savings, causing interest rates to fall. Japanese investors looked abroad for high yields and opportunities to invest their surplus capital—and found a willing and attractive borrower in the American government and U.S. corporations. The large flow of Japanese funds to the United States helped to push down the value of the yen and to push up the value of the dollar. Japanese exports to the United States boomed; exports to other areas also were stronger. During the first half of the decade, increases in exports accounted for about 25 percent of the growth of Japan's GNP. At the same time, the United States accelerated borrowings in Japan, which quickly became America's largest creditor.

But there were other factors involved in Japan's expanding capital exports. Japan's high savings could not have been made available to the rest of the world without a relaxation of government restrictions on outflow of capital—a relaxation that, incidentally, the United States encouraged. Japan's Foreign Exchange Control Law of December 1980 liberalized most cross-border financial transactions. For instance, it paved the way for cross-border leases (that is, the Japanese can buy an airplane abroad and lease it to a foreign airline), which involve billions of dollars in low-cost Japanese financing. Foreign exchange transactions were given a further boost by broadening the number of Japanese eligible to participate in the foreign exchange market. Higher ceilings on foreign asset holdings by Japanese insurance companies, banks, and trust funds announced by the Finance Ministry in 1985 and 1986 opened the way for new purchases of foreign, particularly U.S., securities. New opportunities for the issuance of Euro-yen bonds, the greater use of currency swaps, and the increased presence of Japanese financial institutions abroad also contributed to the outflow of capital. On the U.S. side, the abolition in July 1984 of the withholding tax on interest earned by foreign holders of securities issued in the United States encouraged Japanese purchases of such instruments.

The combined effect of high savings and financial deregulation was striking. Japanese overseas investment increased dramatically. By the end of 1985 it totalled $130 billion, a twelvefold increase from 1980. About three-quarters of total net outflow in 1985 went to purchase foreign bonds (net bond purchases were over $50 billion in 1985 compared to $4 billion in 1980), and roughly three-quarters of those bonds were denominated in dollars. Japanese institutions purchased roughly $20 billion worth of U.S. Treasury bonds and notes in 1985. This amounted to two-thirds of net purchases of Treasury notes and bonds by all foreigners, nearly 13 percent of net new Treasury financing in those instruments. In the twelve-month period ending in September 1986, Japanese investors bought just over 10 percent of all new U.S. bond issues. Without these inflows, U.S. interest rates would have risen sharply, thereby slowing American growth. On the other hand, less capital inflow might have created earlier and greater domestic pressures to reduce the federal deficit.

It is worth elaborating further on Japan's overseas investment, because that nation is today the world's major financial power and America's major creditor. Over the past several years, Japan's long-term capital outflows have consistently exceeded its current account surpluses, which means that Japanese private investors have a conscious policy of investing abroad; foreign investment is not, as some observers argue, simply a by-product of Japan's being forced to dispose of funds accrued as the result of the nation's current account surplus. Many Japanese private investors have borrowed abroad short-term and invested long-term to hedge themselves against a dollar decline and to take advantage of different maturities in different asset markets.

During the past few years, Japanese investment preferences have changed considerably. In 1985 and 1986 over 70 percent of Japanese overseas investment was in bonds. In 1987 that figure dropped to roughly 50 percent as the Japanese bought more equities. In 1987 Japanese investors bought about $11 billion in American stocks compared to roughly $3 billion in 1986, although purchases dried up after the October market crash. Japanese direct investment overseas rose from $6 billion in 1985 to roughly $20 billion in 1987, of which roughly one-third went to the United States. Japanese direct investment in the United States at the end of 1987 totaled over $30 billion—still well below Britain at $70 billion and Holland at $50 billion—of which a large portion was in production and assembly plants. In real estate, Japanese acquisitions in 1987 amounted to roughly $13 billion, over six times the figure for 1985; about three-quarters of this is in office buildings and hotels, the vast majority being in New York, Los Angeles, and Honolulu.

The reasons for Japanese investment in different types of instruments vary. Major investors in fixed-income securities have sought primarily to take advantage of the much higher yield on dollar securities than on yen securities and, for much of this period, of the rising U.S. bond market. Although many Japanese investors have lost money as the dollar has fallen, large numbers of Japanese institutions in 1988 continue to invest in dollar bonds either because they have hedged the currency risk or because they believe that they can benefit from interest rate differentials and that the dollar will stabilize vis-a-vis the yen enough to keep these differentials from being wiped out by a further large fall in the dollar's exchange rate.

Japanese investors in early 1987 found it attractive to buy the very large number of U.S. stocks with a much lower price/earnings ratio (U.S. P/E ratios averaged 17 to 1) than those in Japan (where the average P/E was 60 to 1), enjoyed the high dividends on U.S. stocks compared to Japanese stocks, and liked the breadth, security, and liquidity of the U.S. stock market. Although after Black Monday the enthusiasm for American equities plummeted, it is likely that interest will resume when markets stabilize.

Direct investors are largely Japanese companies that want to locate production or research in the United States in order to be close to changes in taste and technology, wish to participate in joint ventures with U.S. companies, need to build distribution capacity here, anticipate the possibility of U.S. protectionism, or are trying to escape from the disadvantages of the stronger yen to the advantages of a weaker dollar. Those who buy American real estate see it as more secure than property in other nations, cheaper than in Japan, returning higher dividends than in Japan, and benefiting from better depreciation allowances. It is in large measure this diversification of Japanese holdings of U.S. assets that has averted the "dollar collapse" that some observers feared—even when interest rate differentials and bonds became less attractive, the Japanese were broadening their participation in the American investment market.

Japan has emerged as the dominant force in world finance in a remarkably short time. Its net international investment position at the end of 1987 was $240 billion (compared with the U.S. high of $141 billion in 1981), and it has become overwhelmingly the biggest foreign buyer of U.S. securities and property. Because there are a variety of structural reasons for Japan's high savings rate and large capital exports, Japan is likely to continue to be a dominant force in world finance for a long time, even if its trade deficit declines. Japan's tax-exempt savings accounts alone in 1987 totaled $2.3 trillion, more than the entire market capitalization of all American stock markets. By the early 1990s, barring a major rise in oil prices, Japan is likely to have net assets abroad in the neighborhood of $800 billion. Over time, Japan's aging population, which will absorb large amounts of savings, and its weakening trade position (resulting from currency shifts and higher domestic growth) will reduce new savings available for export, thus cutting Japan's current account surpluses and slowing the growth of its net external assets. But that will be largely a matter for future years.

West Germany. West Germany has also become a major exporter of capital to the United States, though on a smaller scale than Japan. Until 1987 both followed similar fiscal policies. In the early 1980s the primary goal of West German fiscal policy was to curb the nation's federal deficit and reduce its public debt as a percentage of GNP. In 1981 public-sector debt accounted for over 36 percent of GNP compared with just 25 percent in 1975. The burden of interest payments on the public debt had risen from 1.4 percent of GNP to 2.8 percent of GNP during the same period. The Kohl government tried to slash these figures by tightening fiscal policy. Although upward momentum pushed government debt to 42 percent of GNP in 1984, it has stabilized at roughly that level. And the Bundesbank's monetary policy has consistently sought to avoid inflation.[6]

West German monetary and fiscal policy is predicated on the notion that excessive stimulus would produce more inflation than growth due to the rigidity of the German labor market and the tendency of wages to rise during periods of inflation but not fall during periods of slow growth. Bonn argues that wage inflexibility, hiring and firing laws that tie employers' hands, and labor immobility present structural problems that tend to make the economy inflation-prone, endanger the nation's competitiveness, and cause management to invest in new capital as a substitute for labor, thereby adding to unemployment.

This rang true in the 1977–80 period, when net labor costs per employee increased by 4.8 percent while real GNP per employee increased by 3.2 percent. But from 1980 to 1986 real labor costs per employee increased by only 4.3 percent while real GNP per employee increased by 13.4 percent, demonstrating a significant improvement in the flexibility of German labor/productivity relationships. Recently, however, unit wage costs have risen, while in Japan, whose currency has strengthened by about the same amount, unit wage costs were lower than a year ago. Moreover, with a well-developed system of railroads, good public and private housing, and well-developed medical facilities, there is very little in the way of public works for the government to finance—in contrast to Japan, with a backlog of unmet social and economic infrastructure needs.

West Germany's household savings rate (13 percent of GNP) is considerably greater than that of the United States. As in Japan, the savings rate substantially exceeds the rate of investment, which has been held down by relatively slow domestic demand. This excess of savings over investment has enabled West Germany to become a large exporter of capital and a large net creditor. And like Japan, West Germany has relied on exports for a significant portion of its growth—roughly one-third of its GNP increase in recent years.

Unlike Japan, though, West Germany has not of late been an exporter of *long-term capital.* In 1986, for example, German purchases of foreign securities declined while foreign purchases of German securities increased sharply. A long-term capital outflow of DM 10 billion in 1985 became an inflow of DM 38 billion in 1986, as German investors shied away from taking dollar currency risks and foreign investors became interested in a strengthening deutschemark. West Germany's capital outflows came mainly in the form of *short-term capital,* which was heavily denominated in deutschemarks to protect investors from foreign exchange losses.

Rest of the World. As noted above, the deterioration of U.S. trade was, with the exception of the Middle East, virtually worldwide.

U.S. trade suffered a nearly $20 billion deterioration vis-a-vis Latin America between 1981 and 1985 as the result of the latter's serious debt problems. U.S. exports dropped by $11 billion due to Latin America's tight foreign exchange situation, and imports increased by $9 billion as Latin America focused more resources on exporting. The newly industrializing areas of East Asia also had a strong effect on the U.S. trade picture. Hong Kong, Taiwan, Singapore, and South Korea have become highly competitive. They have pursued effective export strategies to penetrate foreign markets, particularly the United States. Exports to the United States account for over half of the phenomenal growth in the total exports these countries collectively have enjoyed. In 1985 they together had a nearly $25 billion trade surplus with the United States, compared to a $7 billion surplus in 1981.

East Asian developing countries have benefited greatly from recent movements in currency markets. Since 1985 the dollar has fallen by far more against the major industrialized nations than against the currencies of these countries. Thus the industrialized nations of East Asia have managed to preserve a large measure of their competitive position with respect to U.S. goods, and their products now enjoy a much more favorable competitive position vis-a-vis Japan and Europe.

But lest we be overly preoccupied with bilateral balances—and forget that in a multilateral trading world it is the overall balance that determines whether a country is contributing or not contributing to global equilibrium—it is significant that the current account positions of these countries are very different. Taiwan's current account surplus is significantly larger than that of Hong Kong and Singapore.

3 / The Role of the Dollar

America's trade balance, capital flows, and external debt directly affect, and are affected by, the movement of the dollar. The most visible and direct cause of the weakening of the U.S. current account balance and the buildup of external debt after 1982—although not the only one—was the extraordinary strength of that currency. Between 1980 and 1985, it appreciated by about 40 percent in real terms. Because the dollar's rise was a primary contributor to the worsening U.S. trade and current account balances, and thus to the buildup of its foreign debt, the currency's decline must play a key role in their improvement. (See Chart 5.)

Exchange rates affect the relative price of tradable goods and services and the relative price of financial assets. The movement of currencies is determined by the interaction between the goods and assets markets. Participants in the financial market compare the attractiveness of the financial assets of one country with those of another largely by calculating relative rates of return, inflation differentials and expectations, the overall outlook for various national economies, and confidence in political and monetary authorities.[1] Their decision to buy and sell currencies is directly affected by such comparisons.

If, as was the case in the United States earlier in this decade, a country's domestic interest rates are higher than those abroad, its rate of inflation is declining, its monetary authorities appear committed to continuing to fight inflation, and its politics are stable, then that country's financial assets look like a good buy to foreign investors—particularly if assets denominated in the currency of the country in question represent a relatively low portion of the portfolios of those investors. They then bid up the exchange value of the country's currency in the process of investing in its assets.

For a time, movements in the price of currencies that reflect asset preferences may dominate. But over the longer run, the balance of trade on goods and services will have an increasing influence on exchange rates, because when a country experiences a large annual current account deficit foreign holdings of its assets rise. Then, as investors abroad become uneasy about the growing amount of a country's securities in their portfolios, they are reluctant (unless, of course, that country's interest rates rise to make its securities, for example, bonds, sufficiently attractive) to acquire additional assets denominated in the currency of that country. By reducing or slowing their demand for its assets, they also weaken demand for its currency. If the supply of the currency made available to the world through large current account deficits remains large, and demand for the currency weakens, the currency's value declines.

Chart 5
The Dollar and Real Net Exports, 1970–85

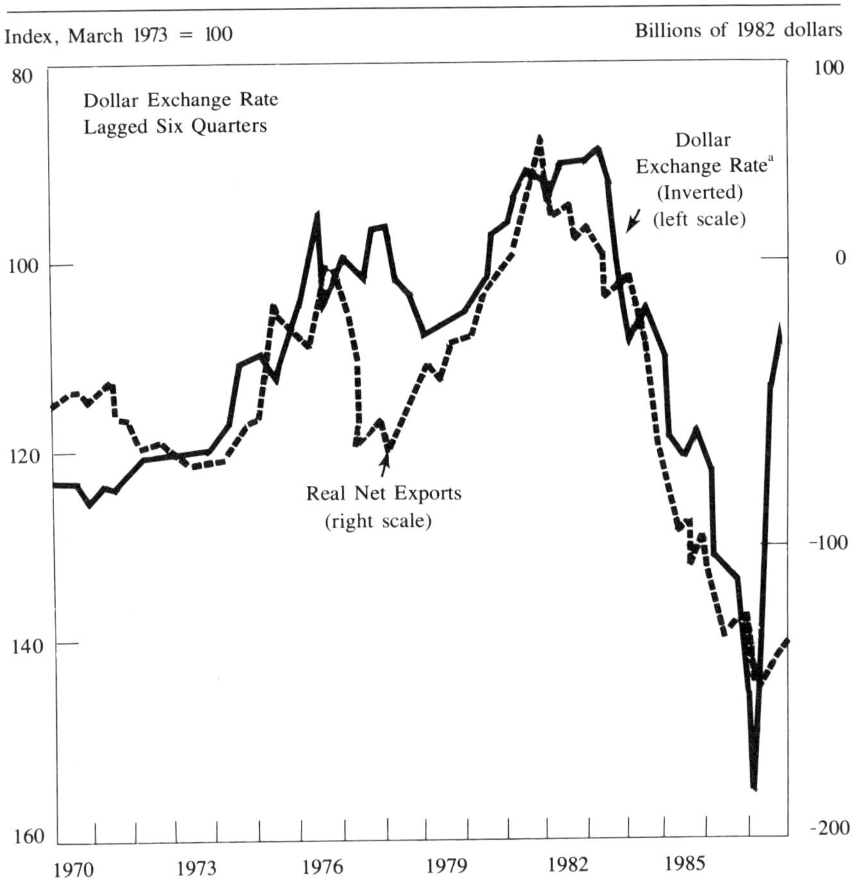

Sources: Department of Commerce; Board of Governors of the Federal Reserve System; *Economic Report of the President,* February 1988, p. 27.

a. Nominal multilateral trade-weighted value of the dollar against the currencies of the other G-10 countries plus Switzerland.

The usual pattern did not take hold as quickly in the case of the United States as conventional economic models suggested it might. In the early 1980s expansionary U.S. fiscal policy coupled with tight monetary policy led to high interest rates. From 1980 to 1982, the interest rate differential between long-term U.S. bonds and long-term Japanese bonds rose from below 1 percent to 6 percent. Even though the U.S. inflation rate declined, and the differentials between its interest rates and those abroad narrowed after 1983, U.S. rates continued to remain high in real terms. What also proved attractive to foreign investors was that through the early part of the decade, as noted in chapter 2, the U.S. bond market enjoyed a large rally; the Federal Reserve allowed rates to fall—as inflation pressures abated—while maintaining the confidence of financial markets that its priority continued to be holding down inflation. That made American assets—particularly bonds and other debt securities—appealing as an investment to large numbers of foreign citizens, despite the rising trade and budget deficits. Thus the growing number of government bonds issued to finance the U.S. budget found ready buyers here and abroad. Moreover, many overseas investors did not see profitable investment opportunities at home.

From 1983 to 1985, despite great progress in lowering inflation in the United States, real interest rates on long-term bonds remained relatively high. In 1983, for example, long-term U.S. bonds yielded over 11 percent. Japanese bonds yielded roughly 7 percent and German bonds roughly 8 percent. The primary cause of this large differential was the current and expected U.S. fiscal deficits, which kept bond rates from falling in line with short-term rates. Americans were willing to pay high real rates of interest in part because, in the words of Martin Feldstein, "the 1981 change in tax rates and the fall in inflation produced a higher real after-tax return on corporate investment in plant and equipment."[2]

Exporters to the United States plowed the growing sums of money they earned from mounting exports to the United States back into the American capital markets. As the value of the dollar increased, overseas investors became increasingly interested in buying dollar securities not simply because of their yield or prospects for appreciation but in order to profit from the anticipated further rise of the American currency and to avoid losses from holding other currencies. The currency market was creating its own momentum. The climb of the dollar to its peak in February–March 1985 was largely the result of this speculative momentum.

The dollar's ascent severely weakened the competitiveness of American manufactured goods. The price of U.S. exports in foreign currencies rose by roughly 50 percent between 1980 and the first quarter of 1985, and at home U.S. manufacturers lost about 25 percent of their price competitiveness vis-a-vis comparable imports. (See Chart 6.) The difference occurred because most U.S. exports are priced in dollars, and as the dollar rises vis-a-vis other currencies the price of American goods in foreign markets increases by roughly the same amount. Whereas foreign producers selling to the United States did not cut their prices in dollars by the same amount as their currencies fell against the dollar—a move

Chart 6
Relative Prices of Exports and Imports and the Exchange Rate, 1975–87

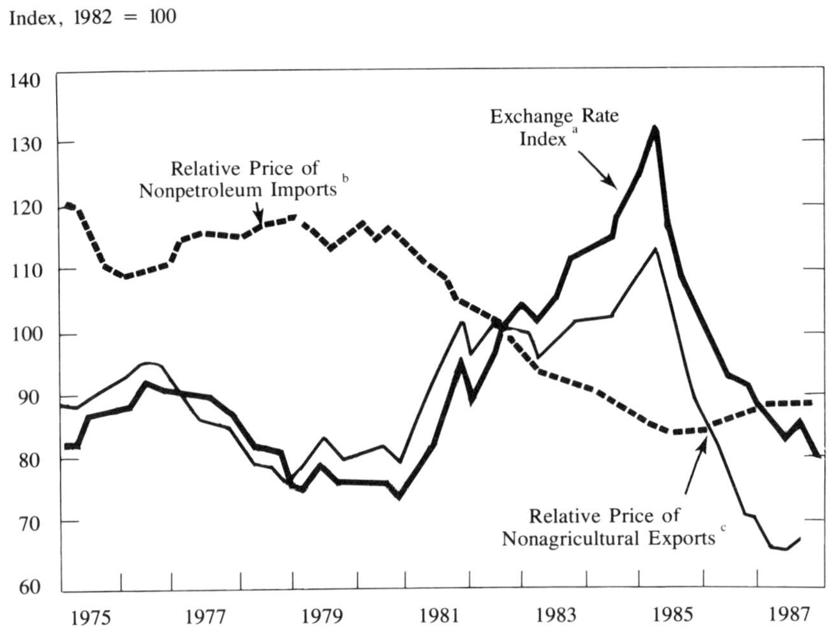

Sources: Department of Commerce; Department of Labor; Board of Governors of the Federal Reserve System; *Economic Report of the President,* February 1988.

a. Multilateral trade-weighted value of the dollar against the currencies of the G-10 countries plus Switzerland.

b. Ratio of the implicit price deflator for nonpetroleum imports to the U.S. consumer price index.

c. Ratio of the implicit price deflator for nonagricultural exports multiplied by the exchange rate index to a GNP-weighted consumer price index for the G-10 countries (excluding the United States) plus Switzerland.

Note: Data for the fourth quarter of 1987 are preliminary.

designed to boost their profits. The U.S. share of world exports dropped from 12 percent in 1981 to below 11 percent in 1985 and remained at roughly that level through 1987. Imports increased by about 60 percent in real terms during that period, rising from 13.5 percent of all imports in the world to 17.4 percent in 1985; that percentage stayed roughly constant through 1987. In 1987, nonoil imports were equivalent to roughly one-quarter of the value of domestically produced goods—nearly twice the percentage of 1980. Exports in that year accounted for only 14 percent of domestic American goods production. In 1981 the U.S. trade deficit stood at $40 billion; by 1986 it had increased to nearly $160 billion; by 1987 it had grown to $171 billion.

These shifts translated into a serious loss of jobs, profits, capacity, and markets for many industries, and particularly for manufacturing—whose exports in volume terms declined by 20 percent between 1980 and 1985, compared with a 42 percent increase for Japan. Those sectors of the economy that were not particularly sensitive to the higher dollar, and benefited from low interest rates, such as housing and nonresidential construction, prospered. The high dollar caused an acceleration of the transition, already under way, of workers from manufacturing industries (where it cost roughly one million jobs) to service enterprises; placed stiff downward pressure on wages, prices, and profits in the manufacturing sector; and intensified pressures for protection.

At the same time, wage and price restraint in many industries helped to offset the adverse impact on their price competitiveness resulting from the higher dollar. And many companies launched major programs to modernize plant, equipment, and management style. Manufacturing productivity rose by 4.5 percent annually from 1981 to 1986 compared with a 1.3 percent average annual increase from 1973 to 1981. Comparable figures for business in general in those years were 1.7 percent and 0.6 percent, respectively—underscoring the degree to which manufacturing productivity increased relative to that in the overall economy. As the 1988 Economic Report of the President put it, "The primary benefit from stronger productivity growth in U.S. manufacturing has been lower unit costs relative to the total private business sector. The reduction in costs has translated into substantial reduction in prices of manufactured products. Between 1981 and 1986 the relative unit costs for manufactured products have fallen by 13 percent, and the relative prices of manufacturing output have fallen by 10 percent."[3] The strong dollar, in short, had created competitive pressures to which American manufacturing had responded by raising productivity.

In 1985 foreign exchange markets began to take a negative view of the dollar. Concerns over the growing magnitude of dollar-denominated financial assets in foreign investors' portfolios, the likelihood of continued large trade deficits and declines in American interest rates relative to those abroad as the U.S. economy weakened helped push the dollar down from its early 1985 peak. In addition, a drop in oil prices benefited currencies of large oil-importing countries relative to the dollar. With the market increasingly of the view that the dollar was overvalued, concerted intervention by European central banks and the Bank of Japan in January and February 1985 triggered a sharp fall in the currency. From February 1985 to August 1985, the dollar dropped by a monthly average of 2.7 percent against the deutschemark and 1.5 percent against the yen.

Private investors increasingly took the view that the interest rate on dollar-denominated securities was not adequate to offset the risk of a sharp fall in the dollar's value to the lower levels deemed necessary to reduce the U.S. trade deficit and avert protectionist trade legislation. And so they became less enthusiastic about the acquisition of U.S. assets and the currency needed to buy them. But for much of 1985 the dollar declined erratically—neither quickly enough nor by a large enough amount to reverse the rising U.S. trade and current account deficits. Nor was there great confidence in the market that it would continue.

In late September 1985 finance ministers and central bank governors of France, West Germany, Japan, Britain, and the United States sought to bring down the dollar's exchange rate more decisively. The Group of Five, meeting in a highly publicized session (a dramatic departure from the relatively secretive approach usually practiced by the Group) at the Plaza Hotel in New York, agreed that "further orderly appreciation of the main non-dollar currencies against the dollar is desirable," and that they would "cooperate more closely to encourage this."[4] The agreement was part of an effort by the United States (James A. Baker III's constructive new leadership at Treasury was especially critical) and its partners to forestall restrictive U.S. trade legislation and to reverse the deterioration of U.S. trade balances. It was also the first time that the Reagan administration had committed itself publicly to cooperate with other nations to manage exchange rates. Deutsche Bundesbank president Karl Otto Poehl called it "the beginning of close cooperation and coordination of economic and monetary policies."[5]

The Plaza agreement's effect on market psychology, plus exchange rate intervention by central banks, pushed the dollar down sharply just after the meeting. But then the slide continued at roughly its earlier pace. Investors recognized that the dollar would need to fall a lot more to reduce the U.S. trade deficit, that current interest rate differentials between the United States on the one hand and Japan and West Germany on the other were not sufficient to compensate for the expected fall, that a weakening of the dollar could cause higher inflation in the United States, and that the Federal Reserve would probably lower interest rates still further in order to stimulate flagging American growth. This *market* view was the main reason for the steady fall in the value of the dollar over the remainder of 1985 and much of 1986. (From October 1985 to 1986, the dollar's monthly decline against the deutschemark averaged 2 percent; its average monthly fall against the yen was 2.6 percent.) Japan helped by raising domestic interest rates in order to encourage the dollar's decline vis-a-vis the yen.

Throughout this period the dollar served as an instrument for both encouraging economic policy changes abroad and directly promoting trade adjustment. Treasury Secretary Baker initially encouraged markets to push the dollar down: "We are," he said on October 23, 1985 (with the dollar at 220 yen), "not displeased at seeing that [decline of the dollar]. . . . I don't mean this to imply that we are satisfied with the results to date." On February 18, 1986, with the dollar at roughly 190 yen, he said he would "not be displeased" if the dollar declined more.[6] Baker also emphasized that unless growth picked up in America's major trading partners—thereby increasing demand for American-made goods and reducing the dependence of other nations on exports to sustain their manufacturing output—the dollar would have to fall further. The administration's strategy was to use the falling dollar to prod other nations to stimulate their economies. When other nations stimulated their economies or when he felt further declines in the dollar were counterproductive, Baker eased up.

There were also fears that the dollar would go down too far. Federal Reserve Chairman Paul Volcker frequently stressed that too rapid a dollar decline could trigger a new round of inflation in the United States. On February 19, exactly one day after Baker's "we would not be displeased" statement, Volcker testified that the dollar "may have fallen enough," and raised the specter of inflation as foreign goods rose in price; he also said that the drop in the dollar threatened "confidence in our own currency."[7] Financial officials of other countries warned that an abrupt fall in the dollar's foreign exchange value could cause their net exports to shrink at a rate faster than could be offset by increases in domestic demand, leading ultimately to a recession in their countries that could slow their imports of American goods. As it turned out both Volcker and foreign critics grossly underestimated the size of the dollar decline needed to improve the U.S. trade balance and significantly overestimated the negative impact of the decline that had already occurred on price stability in the United States and growth abroad.

By early 1987 the dollar had fallen in real terms by roughly 40 percent from its 1985 highs vis-a-vis the major currencies, and by over 30 percent against a broader basket of currencies. Since World War II no major currency had fallen so far in so short a time. (It should be noted, however, that the 1985 peaks were not maintained very long, and they were never really incorporated into trade prices.) According to the Morgan Guaranty Trust, the fall from the 1985 *average* against the currencies of the major U.S. trading partners was about 28 percent.

Despite the dollar's dramatic fall, the corrections expected in the U.S. trade and current account deficits were painfully slow to appear. This was true for a number of reasons.

First, currency shifts lead to improvements in the volume of trade flows by altering import and export prices. Without significant increases in the price of goods imported into the United States relative to comparable U.S. goods and without substantial declines in the local currency price (that is, yen or sterling price) of U.S. exports abroad, trade patterns will not change. In 1986 and 1987 those relative price changes took place slowly. As the International Monetary Fund's *World Economic Outlook* of April 1987 noted: "Prices of U.S. imports other than oil increased by 5 1/2 percent from the first quarter of 1985 to the fourth quarter of 1986, that is, by only about a fifth of the depreciation in the exchange rate over this period."[8] It was only in early 1987 that import prices began rising significantly—at an annual rate of 10 percent. From 1980 to 1985 the price of foreign goods in the United States had declined relative to comparable domestic goods by roughly 26 percent; between 1985 and 1988, the price of imports relative to domestic goods retraced only about one-third of the earlier decline. Import prices remained low because large numbers of foreign exporters chose to try to maintain a large market share in the United States by holding dollar prices low enough to compete with domestic producers rather than protect their their profit margins, when translated back into their home currencies, by raising their prices in dollars. Many foreign companies could afford lower profit margins for a time because of the cushion afforded them by the high profits they had realized during the four years of dollar strength. (See Chart 6.)

On the other hand, the price of most American manufactured exports relative to comparable goods produced abroad fell substantially because American exporters passed along most of the competitive benefits of the lower dollar to the foreign buyer in the form of lower prices in foreign currencies; that is, the Japanese consumer now pays less yen for the goods he buys from the United States than he did two years ago. This has enabled U.S. exports to regain virtually all of the price competitiveness lost from 1980 to 1985.

Developments in the auto sector illustrate the point on import pricing. To generate the same amount of yen in early 1987 as in 1985, Japanese auto companies would have had to increase the dollar price of cars sold in the United States by about 45 percent. But as of July 1987, they had increased car prices by less than 20 percent.

There is, furthermore, a lag between price changes and their effect on orders and shipments. So even with respect to exports, which have regained price competitiveness, trade responds slowly. In some sectors, such as industrial raw materials and forest products, orders are placed all the time and deliveries are made quickly; in 1986 new orders reflecting price changes were already being received and filled, and over the course of 1986 exports of these products increased by 45 and 75 percent, respectively. But orders for large, made-to-order items, such as airplanes, fabricated metal, or other types of capital goods, are normally placed well in advance. Old orders, reflecting previous buyer decisions based on past currency relationships, were being filled throughout 1986 and 1987; newer price patterns only led to actual shipments with a long lag.

And import volumes tend to fall more slowly in response to a currency's depreciation than import prices rise. This so called J-curve effect leads initially to an increase in the import bill of the country whose currency has declined. So as the dollar fell significantly and import volumes declined very slowly, the cost of overall U.S. imports rose in dollar terms. As currencies stabilize, the import bill in dollar terms will more accurately reflect import volumes.

Another reason for slow U.S. trade improvements is that markets for goods do not necessarily follow pure currency models. Perfect symmetry is not a governing factor in international competition. The higher dollar had structural consequences that do not simply vanish because it has returned to, and indeed dropped well below, the levels of 1981—a year when the United States had a current account surplus. The dollar was so strong for so long that some U.S. manufacturing facilities were shut down and capacity was shifted abroad. Many foreign firms enjoyed large profits during this period and plowed them back into new equipment and research, which makes them lower-cost, higher-quality competitors than they were in 1981. Moreover, there is a big difference in the profit level at which a firm chooses to *begin* selling into a market and that which compels it to *stop.* For example, suppose a German exporter decided to enter the U.S. market when the deutschemark was valued at two to the dollar, and he was satisfied that he could then make a 15 percent profit. Once having made that decision, he builds up a distribution system here and invests considerable time and management effort to develop sales. So even if the dollar declines to, say, DM 1.70 he may continue to sell in the United States even if his profits are lower. He may not have chosen to enter the market at that currency level, but it will not necessarily force him to leave. Simply put, his entrance and exit price differ sharply.

To remain competitive in the early 1980s, many U.S. companies increased "outsourcing"—that is, intensified their use of foreign-produced components in domestic final goods in order to lower their costs and remain competitive. For example, until 1980 foreign parts accounted for only 2 or 3 percent of a Boeing plane; today that figure is nearly 30 percent. So even as U.S. exports of major items such as airplanes, computers, and tractors increase, so must imports of the components needed to produce them; to the extent that the lower dollar will encourage U.S. companies to source more components onshore, it will do so only over time.

In addition, key U.S. industries have not traditionally concentrated on exports, and some have recently lost market shares that will be difficult to reclaim. Returning to an example from the chemical industry, the following analysis illustrates the point: "Relative to the Europeans, the U.S. chemical industry is significantly less geared up to export . . . clearly the high [and rising] valuation of the dollar between 1982 and 1985 inhibited exports." There were also structural problems that preceded the dollar rise. "A longer standing factor as far as Europe is concerned is likely to be the relatively limited presence in Europe of many of the major U.S. producers and thus the absence of a well established distribution system through which to channel exports. This of course does not apply to all companies; several major U.S. groups have sizeable operations in Europe. However, during the late 1970s, many other American chemical groups withdrew from, or greatly curtailed, their European production operations."[9] The point is that in this important industry, at least, lack of distribution capabilities and market familiarity inhibits some companies from quickly taking advantage of the lower dollar.

Another problem is that, during the period of the high dollar, disinvestment occurred in many U.S. industries, rendering them less able to take advantage of more market-oriented exchange rates. Further, a number of American companies want to expand their production abroad, regardless of the dollar's value, in order to be closer to foreign customers; indeed, in 1987 U.S. companies' direct investment abroad nearly doubled the figure for 1986. In some very labor-intensive sectors, for reasons having less to do with exchange rates and more to do with the combination of technical advances and lower foreign wages, U.S. producers have lost ground to foreign producers and will not be competitive for the foreseeable future, regardless of the dollar's value.

Moreover, generating new investment in plant and equipment in the United States to boost export capability or increase import substitution in response to currency shifts takes time; the results of the new investment in manufacturing capacity now taking place—which will be discussed later—will not be felt for several years. Complicating the matter further, much of the demand by U.S. industry for new capital equipment to increase output capacity has been filled from abroad; in some cases the reason is that there is no American producer, in others it is that the price of capital goods imports relative to comparable U.S. goods has not increased much since 1985, following a 30–40 percent competitiveness improvement gained by such imports early in the first half of the 1980s. And a number of companies are reluctant to commit new investment capital to build or expand manufacturing capacity in the United States because they believe the dollar may again shoot up in value—an apprehension that is not totally irrational given the enormous swings of recent years. Some investors prefer a production base in a country with a weaker currency and lower wages, such as Singapore or Taiwan.

The question of erratic currency markets also inhibits trade adjustment in other ways. Japanese producers who may feel the need to withdraw from the U.S. market when the yen is 125 to the dollar will hang in longer if they anticipate a sharp upward movement in the dollar; likewise, an American who is considering establishing a program to sell in, say, West Germany will be reluctant to put in the time and money if he feels the dollar will again rise. Thus the history, and future possibility, of currency volatility is itself a deterrent to trade adjustment, as price signals provided by currencies have lost much of their credibility.

The unevenness of the dollar's decline is also a factor slowing adjustment. It has fallen relatively little against the currencies of most East Asian nations, and actually appreciated against the currencies of a number of high-debt Latin American nations. The Dallas Federal Reserve Bank found that as of early 1987 the dollar had fallen by only 16 percent against a broad range of America's trading partners (recall the Morgan figure of a 28 percent decline against a smaller—albeit more significant—group).

There are other reasons why the U.S. trade balance has not improved. The American farmer finds it difficult to boost foreign sales significantly because of the self-sufficiency in grains recently achieved by formerly large import markets, such as India, China, and even Saudi Arabia; he must also face competition from agricultural products subsidized by the European Community and other foreign governments. Nontariff barriers imposed by U.S. trading partners in such areas as agriculture, telecommunications, military equipment and services, and restrictions on government procurement also slow improvements in trade. The inability of high-debt countries to finance large increases in imports, and their aggressive efforts to export more to the United States, also severely hinders American trade with much of the Third World.

Oil has played havoc with U.S. trade. In 1987, the cost of oil imports was about 46 percent above the 1986 level—contributing roughly $50 billion to America's trade deficit. Rising domestic consumption and falling production are likely to lift oil import volume further in coming years. On the other hand, because oil, and other commodity prices, are denominated in dollars, the lower dollar has decreased their prices in yen, deutschemarks, guilders, and lira, thereby lowering the cost to Japanese, German, Dutch, and Italian consumers—permitting them to buy more manufactured or other goods. Lower oil and commodity prices have also helped these countries to cut the cost of production to cope with the lower dollar. As a result, the same product that cost 100 yen to produce five years ago might now cost only 90 yen because of lower energy and commodity prices. Also workers, component suppliers, and engineers in Japan and elsewhere have learned how to improve efficiency, better synchronize component delivery to production requirements, and streamline the distribution process; and many Japanese and European components are imported from lower-cost producers in the Third World.

Finally, it is essential to factor in the question of different growth rates. Strong U.S. domestic demand relative to demand abroad inhibits large improvements in trade. In the United States, for example, consumer expenditures in the first quarter of 1988 grew at an annual rate of 3.2 percent, only slightly below comparable figures in Japan, West Germany, and Britain. How this high demand can affect trade is easily illustrated again in the chemical industry: "At current [1988] exchange rates U.S. manufacturers have an appreciable cost advantage in many products over producers in Europe. . . . This is indicative of the scope for profitable exports of chemicals from the U.S. to Europe. . . . However, the U.S. chemical industry has itself been enjoying . . . high operating rates, demand having caught up with supply after a period of underinvestment. Indeed, so high have been operating rates that availability of many products for export has been curtailed. Overheating in the U.S. domestic market has enabled prices to be raised toward (and in some products above) European prices. . . ."[10]

This example draws attention to the point that domestic policy shifts are needed to validate and enable countries to take advantage of the incentives for the reallocation of trade flows and for the redeployment of domestic resources provided by currency shifts. If a nation's currency declines while domestic demand continues to grow at a rapid rate, incentives for domestic producers to take advantage of improved (currency induced) price competitiveness to boost exports will be diminished because they will continue to concentrate on the domestic market. In addition, strong domestic demand means that prices and wages are likely to increase to the point that they erode gains in price competitiveness resulting from the currency's decline. And the country's appetite for imports will abate very slowly.

Notwithstanding these difficulties, improvements in the U.S. trade performance have finally begun to take place. In 1987 U.S. export volumes grew by 12 percent—nearly three times the growth rate in imports.[11] This occurred despite the relatively high increase (3 percent plus) in domestic demand; it demonstrates the impact on trade of relative price improvements of U.S. goods, particularly exports, owing to the lower dollar and productivity-driven cost cuts. This trade figure represents a turnaround from the sharp drop in export volume from 1980 to 1985.

Comparing 1987 with 1988: exports of chemicals were up 16 percent, basic manufactured exports were up 22 percent, and crude industrial materials (such as wood and pulp) were up nearly 18 percent.

In general, just as manufactured export goods absorbed the brunt of the high dollar, so have they benefited most from a lower one. From the second quarter of 1984 through the second quarter of 1986, the production of manufactured goods (excluding autos and trucks) rose at only a 1.6 percent annual rate; but from the third quarter of 1986 through the end of 1987, manufacturing output grew at an annual rate of over 5 percent. A sort of "Rust Belt Renaissance" is taking place. Many companies in other sectors as well are beginning to realize profits lost during the past several years. IBM indicated that "for the first half of the year, we estimate that the lower value of the dollar . . . has improved 1987 revenues by $1.52 billion and net earnings by $210 billion." A spokesman for the 3M company predicted in 1987 that the lower dollar value "could raise earnings by between $55 million and $70 million."[12]

Many American companies are now in better competitive shape. Between 1973 and 1981, U.S. unit labor costs in dollar terms grew at an annual average of roughly 8 percent; from 1981 to 1987, they grew at an annual rate of 0.6 percent. In contrast, unit labor costs in Japan rose in dollar terms by an annual average of 3.8 percent during this latter period, in France by 0.7 percent, in West Germany by 2.2 percent. This provides hope of further improvements. Moreover, substantial new investment is now planned in sectors such as chemicals, industrial instruments, primary metals, fabricated metal products, and paper—all of which should help the United States to meet rising export and domestic demand without excessive price pressures.

But simple productivity improvements and capacity increases do not in themselves automatically lead to trade improvements. A recent report of the Council for Economic Development noted bluntly that "poor quality and style of the products, inappropriate marketing techniques, and lags in the introduction of new technology into the productive process have also been problems for many U.S. businesses."[13] American industry has made strides here as well, as a new emphasis on quality and customer satisfaction has been adopted in many sectors—but this is an area where further progress is needed.

The Great Dollar Debate

So long as the U.S. trade deficit showed no signs of a significant and steady fall, American officials could not commit themselves to sustained support of the dollar, particularly if doing so meant using large amounts of American reserves to intervene in foreign exchange markets to prevent a further fall. That would have met with criticism by Americans frustrated at the lack of progress in reducing the trade deficit, making it even more difficult for the administration to fight off pressures for protectionism. But Treasury Secretary Baker along with Federal Reserve chairmen Paul Volcker and Alan Greenspan frequently underscored the risk of an excessively large decline in the dollar. They attempted throughout 1986 and 1987 to calm currency markets and, from time to time, to stabilize them around agreed levels, without implying a *long-term* commitment by the United States to any *specific* exchange rate.

Because West Germany and Japan are the most significant U.S. partners from the point of view of their impact on global trade and finance, they have necessarily played a large role in the effort to reduce the U.S. trade deficit and in the debate over how to do it. Much of the discussion between U.S. financial officials and those of these nations in the latter part of 1986 and in 1987 focused on one issue: Had the dollar fallen too far and too sharply? And if so, how should it be stabilized? Leaders in Europe and Japan argued that the dollar had fallen too much, while Washington's position for much of the period was ambivalent.

Meeting in October 1986 Secretary Baker and Japan's finance minister, Kiichi Miyazawa, attempted to convince currency markets that Japan's domestic growth would accelerate and that most of the decline in the dollar and appreciation of the yen had already taken place. Despite the reassuring statements of both men, the market remained unconvinced, and the dollar continued its fall.

Another attempt to achieve stability was made in February 1987 in Paris. Finance ministers and central bank governors of the major industrialized countries, meeting at the Louvre, agreed on a series of domestic policy steps: West Germany was to "increase the size of the tax reductions already enacted for 1988," and Japan was to "follow monetary and fiscal policies which will help to expand domestic demand." The ministers and governors also agreed that the changes that had taken place in exchange rates since the Plaza agreement would "increasingly contribute to reducing external imbalances." Existing exchange rate relationships were referred to as "broadly consistent with underlying economic fundamentals, given the policy commitments summarized in this statement," which was a roundabout way of saying that, if each nation did what it promised it would do, the prevailing exchange rates were basically correct. Further exchange rate shifts among their currencies, they asserted, "could damage growth and adjustment prospects in their countries." In the circumstances, therefore, they agreed to "cooperate closely to foster stability of exchange rates around current levels," implying that they would intervene in the market to stabilize currencies. They also sought to further improve economic policy coordination."[14]

The Louvre agreement helped to reverse the dollar's decline temporarily. It succeeded largely because traders anticipated substantial amounts of exchange rate intervention by central banks if the dollar fell further. Heavy intervention—roughly $70 billion in the first five months of 1987—was in fact forthcoming. But the dollar's decline resumed in the fall of that year as disappointing trade figures and concerns about U.S. inflation triggered a collapse in demand for the currency. In early September the Federal Reserve raised the discount rate for the first time in three years to stop the dollar's decline. The move was, however, not linked specifically to the defense of the dollar, at least in the statement released for public consumption. The decision, the statement read, reflected "the intent of the Federal Reserve to deal effectively and in a timely way with potential inflationary pressures." The Federal Reserve was defending the dollar—without committing itself to a precise rate.

The Louvre agreement proved to be not only a premature attempt at currency stabilization but also a counterproductive one. In attempting to hold the dollar at an artificially high rate, the United States was eventually forced to tighten interest rates. Early in the year the bond market collapsed as foreign investors, anticipating a further fall in the dollar, insisted on high yields for the bonds and notes they purchased in order to compensate them for the expected drop. The firmer dollar also slowed the needed improvement in the international price competitiveness of American goods. Abroad, efforts to hold down the exchange rate of the yen and the deutschemark required massive dollar purchases by the Bank of Japan and the Bundesbank, raising inflationary pressures in these countries. Such pressures, which could have been alleviated by allowing Japan's and West Germany's currencies to rise, added to the reluctance of their governments to accede to American pressures for fiscal stimulus.

Although currency stability appeared to be a reasonable objective, the central unanswered question at the time of the Louvre agreement was "At what level?" With the United States facing a huge trade and current account deficit, it was hard to argue in 1987 that a stronger dollar was appropriate. And yet Washington implicitly encouraged a stronger dollar in the spring and summer of 1987.

In real terms, on a trade-weighted basis against fifteen major currencies, the dollar at the time of the Louvre agreement was just about at the level of 1980. But, as explained earlier in this chapter, that was no guarantee of significant trade improvement. To produce the trade corrections and new investment needed to reduce the U.S. trade deficit substantially, the dollar needed to drop and remain below its real levels of 1980.

Two highly respected economists, David Morrison and Jeremy Hale, of Goldman Sachs, concluded at the time that sustainable equilibrium rates in mid-1987 were roughly 10 percent below those that prevailed at the time of the Louvre agreement—these were roughly 1.65 deutschemarks or 135 yen to the dollar.[15] Martin Feldstein, former chairman of the Council of Economic Advisers, said that the dollar would need to fall by roughly 15 percent below the Louvre rates.[16] Rimmer de Vries, of Morgan Guaranty, argued for a similar decline.[17] The IMF, while not suggesting a specific rate, said that "with exchange rates and domestic policies as they were in early 1987, the U.S. current account deficit would fall very slowly, from 3.3 percent of GNP, its 1986 level, to 3.1 percent in 1987 and 2.7 percent in 1988; this slow decline would cause the U.S. external debt to rise to 8.2 percent of U.S. GNP in 1987 and 10.4 percent in 1988—shooting up to 17 percent in 1991."[18]

The poor trade figures for June, July, and August of 1987 made it clear to the market that the Louvre rates were not sustainable. In the absence of evidence that genuine progress in narrowing the U.S. trade deficit, a further reduction in the U.S. budget deficit, or stronger demand abroad was forthcoming, financial markets looked for a renewed fall in the dollar to produce more substantial trade adjustment. Given inflationary expectations at the time, the markets also expected a tightening of interest rates to stop the dollar's fall. Anticipating this, the stock market weakened in September, as did the bond market. As interest rates crept up in America's major trading partners to offset large increases in the money supply there, concerns about the dollar grew as well, and projections of still higher interest rates in the United States were widespread. These developments set the stage for the October 19 stock market crash, as bond yields by this time had become far more attractive than stock yields.

After the crash the Federal Reserve was understandably unwilling to raise interest rates to preserve the value of the dollar. In fact, it appropriately relaxed monetary policy. The currency fell dramatically in November. That decline was given further momentum because the budget-cutting package put together by the administration and Congress to reassure the financial community emerged only slowly and ultimately proved disappointing to currency and capital markets. Foreign investors were reluctant to reenter the U.S. securities market, and prospects for achieving a significant decline in the U.S. trade deficit continued bleak.

On December 23, 1987, another attempt was made by the Group of Seven (the Group of Five plus Canada and Italy) to achieve "more stable exchange rates." However, they avoided any specific commitment to joint action to support the dollar and did not repeat the phrase in the Louvre agreement to the effect that the dollar's decline since 1985 had brought exchange rates into line with underlying economic conditions. Apparently, the United States was reluctant to commit to stabilizing the currency, which would have implied a willingness to raise interest rates when Washington was concerned about a weakening U.S. economy. The main message instead was that progress was being made to narrow imbalances: "The policies which have been implemented this year are gradually showing their intended effects. In particular, the balance between domestic demand and output in the United States and in Japan and the Federal Republic of Germany has shifted in a direction which promotes external adjustment."[19] There was an implicit understanding that central banks would intervene to prevent a sharp fall in the dollar, but would not necessarily defend a specific target rate.

Economists cannot predict with precision the "right" rate for a currency at any given point, but they can predict with some confidence what will happen if a currency remains overvalued. The longer the dollar stays above a level that (when combined with domestic policy changes) produces a significant and sustained reduction in the U.S. trade and current account deficits, the greater the future growth of U.S. external debt. Put another way, if the trade deficit falls too slowly, the U.S. current account deficit will be swamped by rising interest and dividend payments on funds already invested in the United States—and America's debt will grow at an accelerating rate. The fact that in the first quarter of 1988 the U.S. trade deficit declined while the current account increased demonstrates why the trade deficit must decline significantly more than the outflow of earnings on foreign investment in the United States if U.S. debt accumulation is to be slowed.

Thus the United States appears condemned to a precarious situation for years to come. Unless the trade deficit falls more rapidly, a further weakening in the dollar is likely. American financial officials fear that too sharp a drop will lead to a resurgence of inflationary pressures and higher interest rates. But resisting necessary dollar corrections could delay improvement in the U.S. trade and current account position. That could raise the probability that markets at some point will lose confidence in the dollar, precipitating precisely the type of fall in the currency that the stabilization effort is intended to avoid. Investors would seek a premium on dollar bonds to compensate for the risk of a fall; the resulting increase in interest rates could abruptly slow economic growth. Any way one looks at it, without a steady and sizable decline in the U.S. trade balance, the country is condemned to some combination of higher interest rates and a further decline in the dollar—along with slower growth and higher inflation.

4 / The Costs of Failing to Reduce U.S. Debt: The Experience of Others

Our evaluation of the current U.S. debt situation can benefit from comparisons with, and a historical analysis of, similar situations elsewhere in the world. There are, of course, important differences between America's external debt problem and that of other nations. One key difference is that the external debt of the United States is almost entirely denominated in our domestic currency, which is also the major world reserve currency. Another is that this nation's growing foreign debt poses significant global economic, political, and security risks while the effects of the debt problem of other nations tend to be somewhat narrower in their international implications. But notwithstanding these differences, much can be learned from studying the ways other nations have coped with high external debt. Useful comparisons for this purpose are the Latin American debt crisis, beginning in 1982, and the British debt crisis in 1976.

The Latin American Crisis

In August 1982, Mexico announced that it could no longer service its very high external debt. The nation was suffering from slow export growth owing to the global recession and a higher debt service burden resulting from the rise in world interest rates and massive capital flight. It was paying the price for its enormous domestic subsidies, heavy spending on public projects, excessive money creation, chronically overvalued peso, and rigid domestic economic policies. The immediate response to this announcement was a cutoff of new lending by commercial banks.

In the months that followed, most other Latin American countries—suffering from similar problems—made similar announcements. During that period, commercial banks, Western governments, and the IMF began the frenetic process of putting together emergency "rescue packages" while debtor nations put in place domestic policies to reduce consumption and strengthen their debt-servicing capabilities. New, though very limited, bank lending was resumed, usually in connection with multilateral debt-rescheduling agreements, once these countries subscribed to tough IMF "conditionality" arrangements that involved currency devaluations, tight monetary policy, and greatly reduced government spending. Although this scenario is unlikely to be duplicated in the United States, some parts of it might be replicated, in a somewhat different form.

First, it is useful to consider the differences. Most Latin American external debt is denominated in American dollars and other hard currencies, not in the local currencies of Latin American nations. So the borrower has taken the currency risk. To service or repay foreign debt, Latin American nations must either earn hard currency from exports of goods and services or borrow it from abroad. In 1982, the crunch came for many Latin American nations because they had run out of credit and thus were unable to borrow new funds. As a result, they had to undertake strong corrective policy measures to reduce imports and to earn more abroad through increased exports.

In contrast, as noted above, virtually all U.S. corporate debt and all U.S. government debt are denominated in our *domestic currency.* Lenders take the currency risk. Therefore Americans can simply service or pay off their foreign debts by using domestic earnings. In addition, the U.S. government has the option of being able to tax in its own currency to obtain funds with which to service its debt; it can also "print" money, that is, increase its money supply, and have other nations accept that, at least to a point, as the means of easing the servicing of dollar-denominated debt. Mexico, of course, cannot create dollars; and creating greater amounts of its own currency would do it no good insofar as its external debt service or repayment is concerned because that debt is not in pesos. Nor, of course, can it tax in dollars.

The external debt of the United States is also structured differently from that of Latin America. Individual American companies borrow frequently on domestic and foreign capital markets from a wide range of investors. And the government borrows in dollars in the United States even though significant amounts of the securities it issues are bought by foreign investors. Thus, this country's domestic and foreign debt are intermingled. In contrast, Latin American loans from abroad come largely from banks, which tend to act together in large international syndications, both in reschedulings and in decisions on new lending.

Foreign investors in the United States can also shift funds from debt, to direct investment, to equities or to real estate. In all these areas, markets are deep and varied. If investors are concerned about American inflation, they can move from long-term bonds to Treasury bills or notes. Troubled by capital market instability, they can turn toward less volatile investments in office buildings or hotels. In short, foreign investors in the United States have a wide range of options to choose from. There is, of course, the risk of default by American borrowers. If an individual default is large enough, or if there are several of them, the result could be a short-term pullback of foreign capital from the United States. But unless default were remarkably widespread there would be no questioning of America's national creditworthiness.

The predominant concern of foreign investors in the United States in the foreseeable future is not—as in the case of Latin America—the creditworthiness of the government or of the business sector as a whole, or the inability of the private borrower to have available hard currency in sufficient amounts to service its debts. It is rather a fear that the dollar might fall significantly, leaving overseas investors with less money when their investments are translated back into yen, deutschemarks, or pounds. If foreigners do withhold funds from the United States, they probably will not do so collectively, nor from all American borrowers together, as has recently been done vis-a-vis Latin America. If large numbers of foreign investors should hold back funds, they would probably do so only temporarily, in order to pick up American securities or other types of investments more cheaply after the dollar had fallen to lower levels.

Those are the major differences. But there are a number of similarities between the policies Latin American has employed to cope with its debt problem and those the United States is now adopting to correct its large imbalances. Latin American debtors have had to devalue their currencies sharply to make their products more competitive vis-a-vis comparable goods produced abroad in order to encourage their citizens to curtail imports, spend more of their incomes on domestically produced goods, and redeploy resources to produce more goods for export. In short, Latin American nations have had to export a larger portion of their national output, and consume a smaller portion, in order to reduce the need for foreign borrowing, earn more funds with which to service their external debts, and ultimately stabilize and reduce their debt.

Currency depreciation helped Latin America achieve these objectives. But it also led to a deterioration in its terms of trade. As the peso declined, for example, the earnings and savings of Mexicans could not buy as many goods abroad as they could when it was stronger. Mexico's standard of living vis-a-vis other nations dropped sharply.

Roughly the same thing is occurring in the United States as the lower dollar forces Americans to pay more for cars, television sets, clothes, and other goods made abroad and over time for comparable goods made in the United States. Because the dollar buys less than it did, Americans are finding their standard of living declining vis-a-vis other nations with stronger currencies. In a related development, foreigners whose currencies have strengthened vis-a-vis the dollar can also more easily afford to buy American real estate or U.S. companies, strengthening their buying power of these fixed assets relative to Americans.

Policies to reduce external debt in Latin America usually have been accompanied by a high rate of domestic inflation, as devaluation forces domestic demand to shift rapidly away from foreign and toward domestic goods at the same time that exports are increasing sharply and investment is depressed. This combination has strained existing capacity in some sectors and brought higher prices. Without sufficient fiscal and monetary restraint and higher savings and investment, inflation in many Latin American countries has wiped out much of the competitive benefits of currency declines. Strain on domestic capacity caused by currency devaluation and trade shifts is a problem the United States is beginning to encounter as well; it will become more acute if the United States relies on an ever lower dollar to improve its competitiveness, fails to invest adequately in new productive facilities, and tries to boost exports without restraining domestic consumption.

Many Latin American nations, of course, have suffered a sharp decline in domestic consumption. In the 1970s, most were consuming far more than they produced—the difference being made up by imports financed by money borrowed abroad. As part of the adjustment process, consumption had to be cut back. The United States will also need to slow the growth of domestic spending, which, as was the case in Latin America, now greatly exceeds domestic production. As in Latin America, a decline in consumption relative to production is necessary in this nation to permit a noninflationary expansion of exports.

Up until late 1982, Latin American governments, government-owned corporations, and agencies chose to borrow heavily abroad rather than reduce expenditures or increase taxes. Expenditure reductions would have meant cuts in military capability and politically attractive government social or building programs; higher taxes would have reduced funds available to individuals to spend. When the crisis hit, reductions in government budget deficits through higher taxes and less spending could no longer be avoided. The same alternatives face the United States today. (Ironically, many Latin American nations with far weaker political systems than the United States have moved more boldly to cut government deficits than has the United States.)

Latin American countries that have put the brunt of the adjustment burden on slashing government investment, that is, have attempted to cut budget deficits largely by reducing investment rather than by reducing current expenditures or raising taxes, have, "because of the complementarity between public sector infrastructural investment and private sector investment, inhibited the latter as well."[1] Lower private and government investment, in turn, has limited the capacity of most Latin American nations to meet growing export demand without having to endure severe domestic austerity or intense upward pressure on prices. The long-term consequences of sluggish domestic investment in the United States would be, as in Latin America, an inability to supply additional goods to world markets without increasing inflationary pressures, sharply lower consumption, and thus a considerable decline in domestic living standards.

In order to reduce the U.S. current account deficit and halt the buildup of external debt, Americans will have to put in place many of the same policies used by Latin American nations, while avoiding many of the mistakes they have made. A market-related currency alignment, as the Latin American experience demonstrates, is clearly important to an improvement in the international competitiveness of a nation's goods and an incentive to redeploy production toward exports and import substitution. There is recognition of this in the United States. But this is only the external side of adjustment. The United States has not yet fully come to grips with the domestic adjustment that is needed.

Accepting or promoting a decline in the value of the dollar to boost net exports has appeared less painful to Washington than has reducing the government deficit and easier to the American public than curbing the growth of consumption relative to production. But unless there is a reduction both in the growth of private consumption and in the government's call on resources, it will be difficult to avert inflation as the lower dollar strengthens foreign demand for U.S. goods. Moreover, the lower real interest rates that would result from a reduction in government financing and consumer borrowing would likely lead to more investment in plant and equipment, which is necessary if, over the medium term, the United States is to meet higher foreign demand in an environment of domestic growth and price stability. If consumption and government cutbacks do not occur, inflation will reduce real income as well as the value of savings; one way or another real living standards relative to other nations will decline.

Brazil's experience illustrates this point. In 1985, Brazil shifted from a policy of managing its debt problem largely by reducing domestic expenditures, for the most part by cutting government expenditures, to one that relied almost entirely on deep devaluation of its currency. Initially, growth accelerated, primarily because of the increase in Brazilian exports. But soon inflation shot up, to over 20 percent per month, and real incomes collapsed.

Brazil and most other developing countries now painfully have come to recognize the risk of drastic currency devaluations without complementary domestic policy reforms. Although many political leaders are reluctant to undertake the kinds of expenditure reductions and tax increases that would cut government borrowing and expenditures enough to make a real difference, undoubtedly fearing social unrest from prolonged austerity, they increasingly recognize that without some measures of this sort, currency devaluations will not achieve the desired reductions in trade and balance-of-payments deficits.

Although the situation of the United States is not the same as that of Latin America, the lessons of the latter are important. A relative decline in consumption is the cost of correcting the debt problem. The risk of inflation and a severe drop in living standards is high unless government budget deficits narrow and investment in manufacturing plant and equipment increases.

The British Crisis

In early 1976, Britain was burdened by a seriously unbalanced budget, large trade and current account deficits, high inflation, and an overvalued currency. Britain's Labour government was borrowing heavily at home and abroad. It had accumulated substantial foreign financial debt, although, like the United States today, Britain had (and still has) a very strong international creditor position with respect to direct investment.

In March 1976 the government launched an effort to improve the country's external balances. It engineered a devaluation of the pound from its high of just over two dollars. One reporter described the thinking behind the policy as follows: "If the pound floated downward a few percent, the Treasury devaluers argued, it would make British goods cheap abroad, leading to export-led expansion, a balance of payments surplus and eventually a grand recovery in world confidence in the British economy."[2] The move was triggered by a lowering of interest rates by the Bank of England.

In early March, the pound slipped below two dollars. Then it began to drop sharply—first to the level sought by the government (roughly $1.90) and soon well beyond. Things got out of hand. By June 7, the currency had fallen to $1.71. To stop the pound's collapse, Britain had to take severe internal measures and seek help from the United States and its European partners.

In September, the Bank of England raised its minimum lending rate—similar to the U.S. discount rate—to an extraordinary 15 percent to try to halt the slide. "Political officials on both sides of the Atlantic were numbly aware of the possibility of a bankrupt Britain with inflation fed by unmanageable increases in import costs . . . unemployment rampant as factories closed, and devastating effects on world trade."[3]

A few Labour party leaders proposed a "Fortress Britannia" approach that would have involved import restrictions and capital controls. "Import deposits" (that is, making importers deposit cash at the Treasury in advance of the actual import) would have raised the cost of imports, thereby slowing import growth; in addition, it would have provided the Treasury with additional earnings through the interest on such deposits. The suggestion was opposed by other members of the Labour cabinet, who feared that such a scheme would be deflationary, protectionist, vulnerable to retaliation, and harmful to the Third World. In the end, proposed legislation to impose a system of import deposits was not enacted. The government did, however, reduce military expenditures and foreign aid; it also hinted that "if Britain did not receive the kind of help she wanted, . . . it might not be possible for British troops to remain in Germany."[4]

Pressures on the United States closely parallel those encountered by Britain. A dollar collapse, similar to that experienced by the pound sterling, could be triggered by concern abroad about the uncomfortably high levels of dollar-denominated assets in foreign portfolios, self-fulfilling expectations of a further sharp drop in the dollar, and a possible increase in U.S. inflation. It also could be prompted by foreign fears about problems facing U.S. financial institutions because of their exposure in oil states, real estate, farm loans, and Latin America. Or it could be caused by unexpected political events. In such circumstances, foreign investors might suspend for a period of time purchases of U.S. Treasury securities and corporate debt instruments. They might also sell large amounts of the dollar securities already in their portfolios, which would be even more destabilizing. In Britain, in 1976, foreigners both sold British securities and sharply curtailed purchases of British private and government debt.

But it is not only a drop in *foreign* confidence and *foreign* willingness to hold dollar securities that we should fear. Americans hold more than eight times the amount of dollar-denominated securities that foreign citizens hold. By quickly shifting even a modest portion of their dollar portfolios to securities denominated in foreign currencies, Americans themselves could trigger, or become involved in, a dramatic dollar collapse. The British themselves participated in the sell-off of sterling-denominated securities, although the primary impetus came from central banks and citizens of other countries.

How sharply the dollar would fall in such circumstances would depend on whether foreign investors sought to purchase cheaper dollars soon or waited for a longer time to get even better bargains. U.S. interest rates would rise as the decline in foreign funds being invested in the United States reduced demand for dollar-denominated securities, thereby causing their prices to drop and yields to rise. Interest costs would also increase for the U.S. government and U.S. corporations, because they would have to make their newly issued securities more attractive in order to find buyers (that is, they would need to compensate buyers for expected further falls in the dollar). In the case of Britain, the government had to increase interest rates on government securities dramatically in order to find buyers, at a high cost to the Treasury. At the same time, British import prices increased because of the lower pound; that also led to higher prices for domestic goods and strengthened interest rate pressures.

There was a silver lining of sorts. Britain's trade balance improved steadily after the crisis. Sterling stabilized and strengthened over time, as the market perceived that interest rates had reached a level sufficient to justify the risk of holding sterling assets.

Britain's external debt, and its government's efforts to decrease it, had serious political and security consequences. In extremis, London eschewed the practice of compartmentalizing security, foreign, and economic policies, which it had tried valiantly to do during much of the postwar period. There was a strong body of opinion in the Labour party that foreign assistance had to be cut back to curtail the outflow of funds and reduce the government's borrowing requirement. Aid cutbacks, in turn, weakened Whitehall's hand in a number of developing countries where Britain had traditionally had considerable influence. There also were cuts in military expenditures, further reducing London's capacity to project British power abroad.

Such cuts had important implications for the rest of the world and weakened Britain's international influence. In the case of the United States, the international effect of cuts in foreign aid and overseas military presence would be far more serious.

5 / The Policy Implications of America's Foreign Debt

Rising U.S. external debt poses serious problems not only for current fiscal, monetary, and foreign policy but also for a broad spectrum of national policies well into the future.

Short-Term Implications

Monetary Policy

Big current account deficits require American monetary policy to be extremely sensitive to the need for a smooth inflow of the enormous amounts of capital required from abroad to finance them. By definition, current account deficits must be financed, otherwise they could not exist. But such financing can occur in a disorderly or an orderly fashion—and the difference between the two is the difference between price and capital market stability or instability in the United States.

In testimony to Congress on February 19, 1987, Paul Volcker, then chairman of the Federal Reserve Board, explained that "one potential channel for renewed inflationary pressures would be an excessive fall of the dollar. . . ." He pointed out that "at times during the past year, such exchange rate considerations prompted particular caution in the conduct of monetary policy. The timing of operational decisions with respect to the discount rate or the provision of reserves was affected; on occasion close coordination with the actions of other central banks was particularly important."[1] Volcker was emphasizing that the Fed's decisions on interest rates and credit creation were strongly influenced by its desire to avoid a sharp decline in the dollar and the upward pressure on prices that would result. Volcker also warned that action to reduce growth of the monetary supply "would be called for in a context of strongly rising economic activity and signs of emerging and potential price pressures, perhaps related to significant weakness of the dollar externally."[2]

The Fed, as noted earlier, walks a fine line. Higher U.S. interest rates entail risks for the economy given the nation's large domestic private debt: many American corporations (especially after a surge in leveraged buyouts and acquisitions financed by large-scale borrowing) are highly leveraged, consumer debt is at an all-time high, large numbers of homeowners have a high exposure to interest rate increases because they hold adjustable-rate mortgages, and the farm community (now devastated by a tragic drought) as well as many oil producers (suffering from prolonged price weakness) carry a heavy debt burden. Moreover, American financial institutions are faced with serious problems in their loan portfolios. Hundreds of savings and loan associations, many in the oil patch, are insolvent, and the Federal Savings and Loan Insurance Corporation, whose job it is to bail out depositors if these associations go bankrupt, faces potential unfunded liabilities well above $50 billion.

As Volcker stated in another part of his testimony: "The continuing rapid rate of debt accumulation throughout the economy—running far above the rate of economic growth since 1982—has raised one warning flag. . . . The implicit dangers should be clear. More leveraging of corporations, aggressive lending to consumers already laboring under heavy burdens, and less equity in homes all increase the vulnerability of the economy to economic risk—to higher interest rates, to recession, or to both. The fact that, after four years of expansion, many measures of credit quality are tending to deteriorate rather than improve, and that too many depository institutions are strained, should be warning enough."[3]

Volcker's successor, Alan Greenspan, struck a similar chord: "In the United States . . . we find that non-financial corporations have a very significant proportion of their gross operating incomes devoted to interest payments. It is a number that is rising. . . . If you disaggregate the numbers, what you find is that a very substantial number of corporations in the United States do not have adequate cash flow, not to even mention incomes, to meet debt service charges. We're seeing, as a consequence, a rather significant increase in borrowing to pay interest, which makes a number of American corporations look, to a substantial extent, like a number of less developed countries."[4]

The greater the increase in foreign holdings of dollar securities, the greater the pressure on the Fed to manage monetary policy in such a way that it averts a weakening of foreign confidence in the dollar. A sudden drop in confidence could precipitate a dramatic sell-off. But the high levels of domestic debt noted by Volcker and Greenspan also will inhibit the Fed's use of tight monetary policy to stop a drop in the dollar, because higher interest rates risk pushing heavily indebted firms and financial institutions into bankrupcy. So the Fed will feel constrained to prematurely arrest a dollar decline by raising interest rates. The higher the level of American *domestic* debt, the buildup of which is closely linked to the buildup of this country's external debt, the greater the risk to the American economy of a decision by the Fed to raise interest rates in order to satisfy foreign creditors and to slow the dollar's fall. An increase in American interest rates would also greatly exacerbate the Third World debt problem by compelling debtor countries to spend more of their export earnings on debt service; this would in turn also weaken prospects for an increase in their imports from the United States, thereby slowing the correction in the U.S. trade deficit.

The proper course for monetary policy is most apparent at times when the Fed's currency and domestic policy objectives are compatible. From mid-1984 through early 1986, as well as during the period following the crash of October 1987, the Fed eased monetary policy: U.S. interest rates fell. The Fed wanted to boost growth, and it was willing during these periods to foster, or at least accept, a dollar decline that also helped to stimulate U.S. exports, which in turn provided an added boost to the economy. In the spring of 1987 and then again in the late summer, concern about the falling dollar and Fed worries about higher inflation also coincided, leading to a tightening of credit. However, if the domestic and the external objectives of the Fed become sharply incompatible, for example, if the dollar should plummet while the economy is sluggish, the Fed's choices become extremely difficult.

If U.S. current account deficits continue to be large, foreign investors will tend to seek higher interest rates on dollar bonds to compensate for the fall in the dollar that is likely to occur to narrow those deficits. Early in 1987, foreign purchases of U.S. bonds virtually dried up, contributing to a roughly 30 percent decline in bond values. U.S. long-term interest rates had to increase from roughly 7 percent to roughly 9 percent to make American bonds once again attractive to foreign investors. From an interest rate of 40 basis points below that prevailing on long-term bonds in other major industrialized countries in the fall of 1986, U.S. interest rates rose to a positive differential of 190 basis points, as foreign investors demanded a higher risk premium. Then they dropped back to less than one-half of that level by the summer of 1987, and downward pressure on the dollar resumed. In early and mid-1987 central banks also had to intervene massively in currency markets to support the dollar—but even then its value slipped.

Martin Feldstein, during this period, noted the effects of dependence on foreign capital on interest rates: "The fact that real long-term interest rates are currently twice their historic average reflects the market's concerns that this clash between the government's borrowing needs and private investment demand will soon be exacerbated by a decline in the inflow of foreign capital."[5] A large portion of the American current account deficit in 1986 and 1987 had to be financed by central banks, because private investors would not buy sufficient amounts of bonds or other assets to do so without a major drop in the dollar or sharp rise in bond yields.

Avoiding an Economic Downturn

So long as the United States is heavily dependent on foreign investors to buy its bonds and other financial instruments, it is especially vulnerable to the perturbations of the market. There is constant risk of what C. Fred Bergsten, director of the Institute for International Economics, terms an "investment strike"[6]—an unwillingness for a time of foreign investors to buy American securities. In addition to a natural reluctance to buy dollar securities if they believe that the currency is highly overvalued and interest rates are too low to compensate for an expected dollar fall, foreign investors could also cease buying because of events abroad. For example, a steep decline in the Tokyo stock market, or a collapse in the Tokyo real estate market, which has collateralized part of the meteoric rise in its stock market, could lead to a pullout of Japanese funds invested in U.S. securities. Japanese investors, who have bought stock in Japan with borrowed funds, might need to sell their U.S. securities to cover their positions in Japan.

Alternatively, a shift of Japanese investors away from the U.S. market to purchase more Japanese securities would have a similar effect. In the summer and fall of 1987, for instance, Japanese investors sharply cut back on purchases of U.S. bonds in order to build up yen liquidity in preparation for their purchase of the massive $38 billion NTT stock issue in November; this contributed to a significant increase in U.S. interest rates together with a dollar fall.

Growing external debt must also have an impact on the conduct of U.S. fiscal policy. The growth in federal spending has begun to level off as the impact of Gramm-Rudman-Hollings legislation and curbs on increased military and social expenditures have taken hold. In addition, in 1987 lower unemployment led to reduced payouts of unemployment insurance, inflation-driven cost-of-living benefits declined, lower interest rates slowed the growth of government debt service, and the growth of discretionary programs, such as grants to state and local governments, and revenue sharing was limited by legislation. Outlays dropped from a high of over 24 percent of GNP in 1983 to 22.8 percent of GNP in 1987, while receipts rose from roughly 18 percent to over 19 percent during that period. This stabilizing trend in expenditures, together with rising revenues (in part resulting from transitional arrangements in the 1986 Tax Reform Act and sales of government assets), cut the federal deficit from its record high of $220 billion in fiscal year (FY) 1986 to $148 billion in FY 1987—or by nearly 2 percent of GNP.

The U.S. budget compromise hammered out in late 1987 following the October crash was intended to cut the budget deficit by $30 billion in FY 1988 and $45 billion in FY 1989 from what it *otherwise* would have been. But even with these "cuts," the fiscal deficit appears likely to rise in FY 1989. Were the president and Congress to fail to implement previously legislated deficit reductions in FY 1989, and to go beyond them in 1990 and 1991 (providing the American economy does not weaken to the point that further deficit cuts in those years become undesirable), it could lead to a collapse in confidence in the ability of the government to manage the economy. That, in turn, might lead to a collapse of confidence in the dollar. Moreover, as noted earlier, reducing the growth in domestic demand by narrowing the budget deficit is needed to make room for increased exports without an acceleration of inflation.

If the budget deficit rises as the current account deficit declines (which *ex ante* means a decline in capital inflows), the supply of funds in American credit markets would be stretched. Large government borrowing, plus significant private credit requirements, in the face of a smaller supply of foreign funds would push up interest rates. Government borrowing would then "crowd out" private investment—which is needed to boost capacity to meet growing export demand—because many private borrowers would find it uneconomic to borrow at higher interest rates, whereas the government is not normally bound by such constraints.

Large budget and current account deficits also will make it far more difficult for U.S. officials to cope with the next recession. They increase the probability that that recession will be deeper and more prolonged than it would otherwise have been, because they will make it extremely difficult for the the government to employ traditional countercyclical fiscal policy. Additional spending, or a new tax cut, to "prime the pump" would enlarge an already big fiscal deficit. So the president and Congress might shy away from both. In any case, the fiscal deficit will rise sharply because of a decline in revenues; and legislatively mandated increases in federal social expenditures and unemployment benefits will swell expenditures. Adversely affected domestic sectors also would be less creditworthy, thus reducing the willingness of foreigners to lend to them. In such circumstances, it may be difficult to obtain a steady inflow of foreign financing: and the lowering of interest rates usually counted on to help overcome the recession may be inhibited by demands of foreign investors for high returns on their U.S. investment in order to compensate them for additional currency or credit risks.

Monetary policy will be constrained as well. Given the enormous dollar holdings already in foreign portfolios, and a continued large American demand for imported capital, the Fed might be reluctant to sharply lower the discount rate to stimulate the economy for fear that could bring about a drop in the dollar. Although a drop in the dollar would not necessarily be inflationary in a recession (and the stimulus to exports would in fact be welcomed), it might complicate for a time the effort to finance rising government borrowing, as investors abroad would hold off purchasing dollar assets during the currency's descent.

Foreign Policy

Even before the recent string of large increases in the American trade deficit began early in the 1980s, there were voices urging that the American military presence abroad be scaled down and defense commitments to allies reduced. Budgetary and balance-of-payments considerations—and the higher cost of maintaining troops overseas due to the lower dollar—could lead to a strengthening of those voices and to political pressures for large reductions. Peter G. Peterson, former U.S. secretary of commerce, has referred to this phenomenon as "an austerity led shift toward isolationism."[7]

Domestic arguments that Western defense responsibilities should be better shared within the NATO alliance and with Japan deserve sober and serious discussion. The United States now devotes roughly $180 billion to defense expenditures beyond its borders; $130 billion is for NATO, about the same as the European members of NATO together spend—although the latter also contribute important territory for bases and missiles, more manpower than the United States, and other less quantifiable components. Ten of eighteen standing American divisions are devoted to NATO—five are in Europe and five on standby in the United

States. Pacific defense costs about $40 billion a year, mostly for the defense of South Korea and for the Pacific fleet.

Because political, security, and economic relations are closely tied together in the Atlantic Alliance, the long-term viability and credibility of the defense of Europe depend not only on a strong Atlantic defense system, but also on the close economic and political ties that underpin it. Over time, responsibility for the conventional and nuclear defense of Europe must shift more toward the Europeans. This can be done in part by improving efficiencies in weapons production, research, and interoperability, analogous to the efficiencies that Europe seeks to achieve in 1992 by lowering internal trade barriers. The savings could be utilized to strengthen Europe's defense structure. If this were done in conjunction with a long-term U.S. commitment to maintain a credible presence in Europe, that continent's defense will become more viable, and transatlantic economic and political frictions that could undermine it can be substantially reduced. The danger, however, is that troop-deployment questions will be considered in an emotional environment, in which U.S. public opinion forces cuts in America's overseas military presence with little regard for its impact on Western security. Accusations of unfair foreign trade practices and concerns about the budgetary cost of the U.S. contribution to Western defense could divert attention from broader security considerations. That could create an atmosphere in which the United States threatens to cut its troop presence as leverage to force economic concessions from Europe, or simply scales back its forces out of pique.

Acrimony on this issue within NATO is harmful in the best of times. But following on the heels of the 1988 agreement to eliminate intermediate-range nuclear (INF) weapons in Western Europe—thereby increasing the importance of a continuing American conventional presence and the credibility of America's nuclear commitment to Europe's defense—any talk of a unilateral U.S. troop reduction (much less actually carrying out such a move) could be exceptionally dangerous.

The INF agreement, coupled with growing U.S. domestic pressure for a pullout of troops, could weaken political forces in Western Europe that have traditionally been supporters of close military and political cooperation with the United States and are the strongest defenders of America's military presence in Western Europe. Many of them see INF as the beginning of American detachment from Europe's defense. Unilateral troop withdrawals, real or threatened, as opposed to a negotiated reduction in the context of a larger Western European defense program, coupled with a broader sharing of NATO decisionmaking, or genuine reduction in Soviet conventional forces and short-range missiles, would cause a further loss of confidence in the United States by America's closest friends.

Some experts argue that a unilateral move to cut troop levels would push, or "shock," Europe into strengthening its own defense efforts. But that move could also render Western Europe—concerned as it probably would be about American abandonment—less able or less willing to resist tendencies, already strong on the left in West Germany and Britain, to seek greater accommodation with the Soviet Union on the basis of unilateral force cuts. In Germany, especially, the Kremlin would likely play up the notion, already advanced by Gorbachev, of a "common European house"—implying denuclearization, quasi-neutralization, and closer ties between the Federal Republic and the German Democratic Republic.

Unilateral U.S. troop cuts, or threats thereof, would certainly increase the difficulty (already demonstrated to be great) of developing a Western consensus regarding actions to preserve the peace in the Middle East, resist Communist pressure in Central America, or react firmly in the face of events similar to the invasion of Afghanistan or declaration of martial law in Poland.

The longer large imbalances in the U.S. current account last, and the more difficult they are to reduce, the greater the pressures in the United States will be to cut back America's global military presence or use the threat as leverage to force trade or other economic policy changes abroad. On the other hand, too heavy handed an American attempt to reduce imbalances or obtain trade concessions abroad could prompt retaliatory reactions. The greater the friction over such issues, the greater the peril to Western alliances.

In the Pacific, there is a danger that pushing Japan to increase its military expenditures or putting it in a position where it feels forced to build a large military establishment will lead to excessive militarization. The possibility of an abruptly diminished U.S. security presence in the region might lead some Japanese leaders to conclude that they had to dramatically increase the size and scope of their military, and broaden the geographical range of its presence. It is hard to predict with great confidence what forces might be triggered by excessive U.S. pressure on Japan to increase its military or by a perception in Tokyo of American military unreliability. Much as there is reason for Japan to take a somewhat greater security role in the region, such as defending regional sea lanes, to push too hard in the name of burden sharing without thinking through the consequences and without discussing the issue fully with Japan and her neighbors, or a pull back U.S. forces simply to save money, would entail major risks for the United States, and have powerful geopolitical implications for the entire region.

Concerns over budget and payments imbalances also affect foreign aid. Despite the effort of every American president since Franklin Roosevelt to defend them, foreign assistance programs have progressively lost support in Congress and among the American people. Virtually all of America's allies provide a larger share of aid as a percentage of their GNP than does the United States. Yet opponents of aid programs in this country still charge that the United States is doing more than it can afford to do in this area and that other major nations are providing too little aid relative to the size of their current account surpluses or GNP.

Large additional cuts in U.S. foreign assistance would reduce further American influence in much of the Third World. They would make it difficult for this nation to respond to friends abroad suffering from economic difficulties, as in Central America, or to help faltering democracies, such as the Philippines, threatened by instability or insurrection. A reduction in foreign aid also might tempt some nations to succumb to economic enticements from U.S. adversaries. For example, some small Pacific islands might accept Soviet aid in return for granting the Soviets base or refueling rights. And many American base rights negotiations, such as those with Portugal, depend on substantial payments from Washington. Moreover, for many of our allies, aid is either directly or indirectly linked to exports, so U.S. cuts open up new trading possibilities for many of America's most active industrialized nation competitors.

A number of the big capital-exporting countries among America's allies should be providing considerably more economic aid, especially aid not tied to export-promoting activities. If America pulls back dramatically from bilatcral and multilateral aid commitments, these allies *might* be induced to up their aid levels. That should certainly be a U.S. objective. But if they do not, and so far there is little evidence of their willingness to provide significantly more assistance, (although their share of the World Bank and similar institutions has risen gradually over the years and Japan recently has announced plans for a new $50 billion aid program), there is danger of a collapse of the international foreign assistance effort. If this should happen, the risks of a sharp fall in Third World economic activity and a weakening of political stability in many developing nations become substantial.

Moreover, the Soviets are now beginning an active and innovative effort to forge better relations with developing nations; last year they suggested at the United Nations that funds freed up by future cuts in arms be transferred to the Third World (notwithstanding Moscow's own deplorable aid performance). Cuts in U.S. and Western aid at precisely the moment when this Soviet effort is gearing up will make Moscow's public relations job a lot easier.

The pressures created by large trade and current account deficits are clearly seen in U.S. trade relations. Today, there is no strong U.S. constituency for free trade. By contrast, those economic sectors facing intense import competition are vocal and highly organized. In 1988, Congress passed a bill that tightened up U.S. trade law primarily by creating the strong presumption that the president would take tougher action against trade practices regarded by the United States as "unfair," and reducing his discretionary authority to avoid such actions. Although it was not as restrictive as many observers had earlier anticipated, it did prescribe stronger measures against countries deemed to be imposing barriers harmful to U.S. interests.

Most members of Congress acknowledge that however tough new U.S. trade legislation may be, it alone will not greatly reduce America's trade deficit. Still, many congressmen and leaders of the business community correctly point out that barriers to American goods and services do exist abroad, and that the large U.S. trade deficits of recent years made it both appropriate and necessary for Washington to work especially actively to eliminate such barriers—even if their impact on the trade deficit is modest. Many of the most ardent proponents of free trade, who recognize fully that macroeconomic causes are far more to blame than trade barriers for the trade deficit, and freely acknowledge that the United States has trade barriers of its own, have stressed that at a time when the U.S. trade imbalance is so large, foreign barriers to American goods are particularly unjustified and intolerable—and that the United States should resolutely seek their removal.

Trade tensions can be expected to grow in coming years because of the sheer size of recent U.S. trade imbalances, the magnitude of the shifts in trade flows needed to reduce them, and the likelihood that other countries will seek to resist such shifts by imposing new trade barriers or providing subsidies to domestic producers. We have already seen demonstrations in South Korea and Taiwan in opposition to U.S. pressures for them to further open their markets.

Trade disputes have demonstrated that they can trigger major volatility in currency and capital markets. In April 1987, when the United States announced sanctions against Japan for dumping semiconductors in this market, the dollar fell sharply, the bond market dropped like a stone, and the Dow Jones Industrial Average was off eighty points in one day. Similar market disruptions might result from further trade confrontations, and the market's perception that they could cause an interruption, however temporary, in the influx of foreign capital into the United States.

While much of the discussion in world trade forums seems to focus on, and indeed exaggerate, protectionist pressures in the United States, other nations have high barriers of their own. It is high irony for critics abroad to imply that the United States cannot improve its trade balance significantly because it is no longer competitive in many sectors, while their governments at the same time are providing subsidies, and imposing barriers, in precisely those sectors—agriculture, telecommunications, services, military equipment, and aviation—in which the U.S. products are highly competitive. The Uruguay Round of trade negotiations holds promise of progress toward a more open trading system in these and other areas. But progress will not be easy.

Longer-Term Implications

Large current account imbalances—and the federal borrowing that in part caused them—have serious medium- and long-term implications for American policy and American interests. In the 1970s, interest payments on the federal debt averaged 1.4 percent of GNP. By 1987, these same payments had risen to over 3 percent. And a growing (albeit still small) portion of the interest is now owed to citizens of other nations. Interest payments on the federal debt will limit future U.S. government spending on public services, defense, and social programs—unless, of course, there is an increase in taxes, which will limit the rise in future disposable income of individuals. Further, were spending in such areas as education, job training, and research to be cut back, that would affect adversely the long-term competitiveness of the United States.

Also of critical importance is the damage that continued large payments imbalances will do to the international credibility of the dollar. The use of the dollar as the world's major reserve and transaction currency, and the currency in which a large portion of borrowing by Americans and many others as well is denominated, is a major convenience to American importers, exporters, lenders, and borrowers. But the dollar's sharp decline, and its recent dubious distinction as the most volatile of the world's major currencies, has caused a gradual shift by investors away from that currency. Lenders of funds, such as Japanese insurance companies and pension funds, have reacted to currency losses from holding dollar-denominated securities by seeking to buy more securities denominated in their own and other currencies; and, understandably, borrowers tend to issue securities in currencies attractive to lenders.

In 1982, 82.5 percent of Eurobonds were issued in dollars, 1.6 percent in pounds, 10 percent in deutschemarks, and 0.9 percent in yen. In the first half of 1987, dollar-denominated issues plummeted to 38.4 percent, while pound issues rose to 10.8 percent, deutschemark issues to 16 percent, and yen issues to 19.4 percent[8]. In an atmosphere of continued dollar weakness, or great uncertainty surrounding its value, the financial role of the dollar is likely to be far less prominent than in past years. If private investors abroad shy away from dollar securities, a high portion of American corporate obligations will have to be denominated in currencies other than the dollar, and U.S. borrowers will increasingly have to accept the sort of currency risk that most borrowers in other nations have long had to cope with.

A related trend is the increase in the strength of non-American financial institutions. Japanese commercial banks and securities houses, and the large German banks, are often the preferred intermediaries between investors in their nations and borrowers abroad. Because of the large pool of investable funds in their home countries, Japanese and German institutions are in an excellent position to underwrite large stock and bond issues—a substantial portion of which they can sell in their high-savings home markets—and build a major presence in offshore capital markets such as London and New York. The enormous international market share of Japanese commercial banks, now the most powerful in the world, with gross external assets of over $1 trillion, nearly twice that of U.S. banks, is directly related to the financial resources of the Japanese economy. Japan accounts for seven of the world's ten largest banks. The growing global role of the German banks is likewise related to Germany's financial strength.

These developments all have long-term implications for the U.S. role as a world power. Increasingly, American and non-American investors and borrowers will look to German, Japanese, and other foreign institutions to meet their financial needs, adding yet one more area in which the United States will become more dependent on other nations. Moreover, the U.S. banking system has been the financial intermediary and source of information and contacts, for many small- and medium-size American firms; the relative decline in the international role of many American banks, or indeed the outright pull back from international activities of some, deprive a part of American industry and certain regions of the country of a powerful instrument for pursuing their business abroad.

Longer-term trade problems will also confront the United States if pressures to reduce current trade imbalances lead America's major trading partners to turn inward. The European Community, for example, hopes to complete the process of eliminating internal impediments to intra-European commerce by the end of 1992. If the United States is seen to be erecting new trade barriers, or taking what the Europeans believe to be an excessively tough line on trade to reduce its trade deficit, or if the pressures of trade adjustment imposed by the lower dollar and greater competition from the newly industrialized countries give rise to a protective reaction in Europe, the EC's arrangements could be structured in such a way as to lead to higher effective barriers to United States and other non-European goods. Moreover, as the world's largest market, the EC could hurt American exporters were it to threaten to curtail access to its market in the name of "reciprocity" in order to attain greater access to the U.S. market for European products.

Were the United States to limit imports from Latin America, these nations might conclude that they were justified in taking unilateral action to change the terms of existing debt repayment schedules on the grounds that American protectionism rendered them less able to earn foreign exchange needed to service their debt.

An intensification of trade disputes would also have a strategic impact. If the United States were to strike bilateral or regional deals that impose restrictions on the goods of other nations, rather than strengthen the multilateral, nondiscriminatory rules on which trade, for the most part, has been based for forty years, the trading system will begin to fragment amid charges of discrimination. Trade distortions will abound, leading to political friction. The tendency for regional trade blocs to form would also intensify. For the United States a more divided trading world would be a further blow to its influence in the global economic system—as other nations would have more power in their respective geographical areas.

And there is an East-West dimension as well. For years, one of the major goals of the Soviet Union has been to create divisions between the United States and its Western European and Pacific allies. An Atlantic or Pacific trade war would provide a fertile environment for Soviet diplomacy. Moscow would doubtless offer Western European, Japanese, or other Asian companies the lure of further trade with the East—however small that may be in relation to intra-Western trade—to offset at least a portion of trade lost with the United States, even though the Soviets and other Eastern European nations—having little foreign exchange—would seek enormous, subsidized credits from Western governments to finance these imports. They also would see the trade difficulties between Western Alliance nations as an opportunity to accomplish political objectives impossible to achieve in an environment of harmony among allies, seizing on divisions on trade to argue for closer European and Japanese ties to Moscow, or at a minimum to foster the notion that this was just one more example of the United States turning its back on its allies.

Even assuming more benign Soviet intentions, trade friction between the U.S. and its allies poses problems. For the next several years there will doubtless be a rethinking of East-West trade relations. One of the West's greatest assets vis-a-vis the Soviet Union and China today is its economic and technological strength. Both Moscow and Beijing understand that the market-oriented Western economic system is far more successful than the statist system that has failed their own nations. The way to strengthen the trend toward market-oriented policies in these countries is not by economic lectures from the West but by our continuing to pursue successful market-oriented strategies that promote growth and improved living standards. Trade wars, or other disruptions, would diminish the attractiveness of the Western economic example. The West now has an opportunity to gradually integrate socialist economies into the global system of rules, responsibilities, and benefits, which can both support their reforms and introduce greater predictability and stability into East-West economic relations—adding yet another dimension in the effort to improve political ties. If, however, Western economies are constantly at odds with one another over trade, and indulge protectionist pressures by erecting new barriers to imports, the attraction of such integration for China and the Soviet Union—and thus the willingness of these countries to make accommodations to Western rules and practices—will be diminished. Instead, these nations are likely to seek bilateral trade deals with individual Western nations, thus adding to the fragmentation of the system.

While global trade imbalances result in part from America's lateness in coming to grips with the reality that it cannot indefinitely consume more than it produces, or invest more than it saves, there are other factors as well. The economic strength of America's economic partners in the Atlantic and Pacific—the prosperity of which was a key goal of

America's postwar and post-Vietnam policy—has given rise to greater competition for the United States. This in itself was to be expected as these nations propsered. But many of the most successful of America's allies and trading partners have been slow to recognize that there is a limit to the extent to which they can rely on ever-expanding exports to the United States. Europe, Japan, and the Third World now need to work out with the United States a more pluralistic responsibility-sharing relationship to ensure global growth and balance in the years ahead. If the United States perceives other nations blocking or slowing progress toward reducing its trade deficit, and responds by throwing up new trade barriers, the prospects for maintaining an open world trading system will plummet. Other nations will find this more harmful than the United States—although the United States, of course, will be hurt as well. Political friction surely will accompany this deterioration. And currency volatility, as well as uncertainty about the value of the world's major currencies, will complicate future trade and investment decisions throughout the world.

To sum up, the growing U.S. external debt poses serious economic, foreign policy, and security problems. If America's external debt were to continue to grow rapidly this country would be vulnerable to periods of currency and market volatility and face a diminished capacity to lead the free world and protect its global interests. Large payments imbalances, and heavy dependence on flows of external capital, impose constraints on America's monetary, fiscal, and foreign policies, increase pressures on American trade policy, and jeopardize attainment of U.S. security objectives.

The point is made by some academicians that in a genuinely interdependent world economy, large payment imbalances among nations are no more to be feared than, say, a payments imbalance between Ohio and Michigan, and that market forces will inevitably rebalance the system over time. So, why worry? The difference is that Ohio does not have to contend with a host of global security, foreign policy, and foreign assistance responsibilities critical to the interests of its citizens and those of other regions as well. Nor does Ohio have a separate currency and the responsibility to run a domestic economic policy that depends on the willingness of millions of Michiganders to purchase assets denominated in that currency. The comparison is hardly one that addresses current economic and geopolitical realities.

6 / Curbing the Buildup of America's Foreign Debt

Developing a set of policies at home and in conjunction with our trading partners to slow and then stop the growth of America's external debt has proved difficult, but forces are moving in the right direction. On the positive side, the U.S. budget deficit has fallen sharply; Japan has relaxed its previously tight fiscal policy and achieved vigorous growth in domestic demand; economic activity has picked up in Canada, Britain, West Germany, and other parts of Europe; stimulative monetary policies around the world have helped bring interest rates down following the October 1987 stock market crash; and the international price competitiveness of U.S. goods has improved due to currency change and increased U.S. manufacturing competitiveness. As a result the volume of America's exports has increased sharply while the growth of its imports has slowed.

On the negative side, the U.S. trade deficit in 1987 reached $171 billion—a historic high; and despite significant improvements in mid-1988, that deficit is likely to remain large for the year as a whole. A big trade deficit and rising interest payments on funds previously borrowed will cause America's current account deficit to remain above $140 billion in 1988 and well above $100 billion for the next several years. And so substantial increases in America's external debt loom on the horizon.

Wrong Roads

The long string of large monthly U.S. trade deficits has created political pressure for bold action by Washington. Other countries in similar circumstances have resorted to extreme, often ill-conceived, measures. Some of these are now being considered here.

One school of thought—less prominent in 1988 than in 1987, when trade deficits were growing—calls for the U.S. government to talk down the dollar, or by other means precipitate (or acquiesce in) a sharp fall in that currency. Doing so would clearly improve the international price competitiveness of American products. And getting all of the drop "behind us at once," it is suggested, would eliminate the currency risk of holding American securities; it would thus tend to induce more foreign purchases of U.S. stocks and bonds, with the latter contributing to lower interest rates.

But there are costs to such a strategy. Economists who support it tend to forget that markets often "overshoot," as the dollar did on the up side in 1984 and 1985. Once a big drop begins, it may be hard to stop at the "optimum" level (and in any case, economists disagree on what that level is). Moreover, a significant decline over a few months would likely lead to higher domestic inflation resulting in higher interest rates. The United States could be pushed into a recession before substantial trade benefits were realized. Excessive reliance on a lower dollar also diverts attention from effecting fundamental internal policy changes—for example, a cut in the budget deficit and further productivity increases—needed to improve America's ability to increase exports without triggering higher inflation. While a lower dollar provides a powerful incentive to redirect trade flows and investment, it cannot be relied on wholly to do the job.

In addition, Europe and Japan would react adversely if they believed that Washington had engineered a *contrived* dollar decline (that is, one not in their view justified by market conditions). Believing such an action to be a heavy-handed attempt to undermine the competitiveness of their goods, or to intensify pressures on them to stimulate additional domestic growth, many of America's trading partners would be less willing to cooperate with Washington on international economic matters—for instance, in the current Uruguay Round of multilateral trade negotiations—or on foreign policy issues. In addition, most would be unable to boost domestic growth fast enough to offset the weakening of their exports. As a result, their economies might slow precipitously, eliminating part of the potential export benefit of the lower dollar for American producers. Some foreign governments might respond by subsidizing their nations' exports, or restricting imports, to make up for the sharp loss in competitiveness. And confidence in the dollar's future stability would be undercut by a perception that the United States would *deliberately, and excessively,* weaken its currency as a matter of policy.

Another possible course of action—the opposite of the first—is to artificially stabilize the dollar on the basis of the argument that it has fallen far enough to promote continued trade improvement and that a further decline, particularly a sharp one, would be counterproductive to this effort. That approach runs a risk of holding the currency for too long at a higher level than justified by economic, or market, fundamentals. Although those particularly concerned with the effect of a declining dollar on U.S. inflation might tend to favor an early effort to promote stability, in its own way it could be as harmful as the first course.

Stabilizing the dollar prematurely, without evidence that the U.S. trade deficit will continue to decline significantly in the period ahead, would inhibit trade adjustment by delaying improvements in the international price competitiveness of U.S. goods. It would prevent the currency from reaching levels that would trigger price increases of imported goods sufficient to reduce further the share of these goods in the U.S. market and delay "exit" decisions of marginal foreign suppliers; it would also lead to postponement of decisions to build the new plant and equipment in the United States that are required to meet additional export demand and to produce goods to substitute for imports.

The effort to preserve an overvalued dollar could also lead to higher U.S. interest rates, as demonstrated by the surge in rates that accompanied the premature effort to stabilize the currency in early 1987. In contrast to the scenario described above, interest rates under this approach would rise not because of inflationary pressures but because an artificially high dollar over time would lose market credibility; therefore potential buyers of dollar securities, recognizing that the dollar will *ultimately* have to drop in order to shrink the U.S. trade imbalance, would demand a high interest premium to compensate for this currency risk, or they would hold off buying dollar securities until the currency falls, permitting them to purchase dollars and dollar securities at lower prices. Large-scale currency intervention to stabilize the dollar abroad would lead to an increase in foreign money supplies and so, perhaps, to renewed inflationary concerns in Europe and Japan.

Foreign governments that see currency stabilization as an answer to their worries about a weakening of their trade balances would find that it could—if attempted at too high an exchange rate for the dollar—produce a severe slowdown in American growth as well as higher inflation in their own economies. At best it is merely a device for postponing adjustment; and it would carry the risk of major distortions.

A third approach, although one that has received relatively little support to date, is for the United States to reduce its trade deficit at a more rapid pace by erecting protectionist barriers and increasing export subsidies. While tempting to those who believe that the "playing field is not level," this approach would, *inter alia,* lead to a significant increase in domestic prices. Higher interest rates would follow. And, because many American manufactured products depend on imported components, a wide range of U.S. producers would be harmed. Protectionism would also invite retaliation.

Other countries, alarmed at the prospect of losing a large share of their U.S. market and suffering from high unemployment, would likely respond by imposing restrictions of their own. The European Community, now in the process of constructing a single internal market by 1992, and establishing conditions of "reciprocity" for access by foreign firms to its market, would be likely to react by erecting new impediments to U.S. goods. Such a course would also lead to turmoil in currency and capital markets, serious political friction between the United States and its partners, and a possible breakdown of the world trading system. U.S. barriers to imports would also make the Third World debt problem harder to manage; if developing countries have their exports disrupted by protectionism, they would be less able to service their debts; in an extreme case, they might be driven to default.

The final wrong road would be for the United States to attempt to inflate its way out of the problem. Other nations with large debts have tried to do so by, in effect, eroding the value of their currencies, thereby easing repayment of outstanding foreign and domestic debt denominated in their domestic currency. Such a strategy, of course, would entail enormous costs, among them the loss of hard-won American progress in reducing inflation, a sharp run-up in interest rates, a return to the "stagflation" of the 1970s, and a dramatic reduction in confidence in the dollar and in the U.S. government.

A More Promising Path

Western governments have not yet fully digested the magnitude of shifts in world trade necessary to reduce global imbalances—shifts that necessitate more effective coordination of underlying policies.

A country cannot indefinitely consume far more than it produces, save far less than it invests, and expect to finance the difference abroad. American public opinion will have to come to grips with the notion that the United States must bring its account book into better balance; this requires a period of slower growth in consumption and higher growth in both savings and productive investment. Japan, West Germany, and several of the newly industrializing economies in East Asia cannot expect to rely as heavily on export-led growth in the future; they must instead permit domestic demand to grow more rapidly than domestic output for a sustained period of time (that is, more of their domestic demand must be supplied by imports). One way of doing this is for them to devote more budgetary and private resources to meeting unfilled social and infrastructure requirements in ways that productively engage currently underutilized labor forces. In the process they must accept greater responsibility for maintaining equilibrium and growth in the world economy.

The magnitude of the adjustment required in the world economy in order for the United States to achieve, or even approach, trade equilibrium is enormous. In 1987 the U.S. trade deficit ($171 billion) was nearly 4 percent of GNP—that is, domestic consumption exceeded domestic production by an amount equivalent to 4 percent of GNP, with the difference being supplied by imports. So to eliminate America's trade deficit, production in the United States must expand relative to consumption by an amount equivalent to about 4 percent of GNP. To achieve this goal by the end of 1992—the last year of the next president's first term—U.S. production must grow annually by about 1 percent more than consumption, thereby increasing net U.S. exports (net exports are gross exports minus gross imports) annually by about 1 percent of GNP. America's trading partners, at the same time, would need collectively to increase domestic demand over domestic production by that same $171 billion; that is, as U.S. net exports increase, foreign net imports would have to increase by that same amount.

But that scenario addresses only the trade deficit. It would still leave a current account deficit of about $60 billion in 1992, because the string of annual current account deficits incurred by the United States in the intervening years would have led to roughly $900 billion in U.S. external debt, on which interest and dividends would have to be paid. If the U.S. external debt were to be *stabilized* (that is, its growth were to be halted) at the end of 1992, the United States would have to achieve a *surplus* on tradable goods and services equal in magnitude to the net U.S. deficit on interest and dividend income—that is, a trade surplus of roughly $60 billion. That would mean a trade improvement not of $171 billion relative to 1987 but of about $230 billion. Other countries would have to relinquish trade surpluses of equivalent magnitude. As Carlo DeBenedetti, chairman of Olivetti, put it, "We have all, in Europe and Japan and Asia, expanded on the shoulders of U.S. consumers during the last five years. Now it is our turn to suffer."[1]

Foreign governments and investors could, of course, together finance U.S. current account imbalances beyond 1992, and thus put off the day of reckoning. But that has a cost. If the U.S. current account imbalance remains large enough to discourage private financing, then large-scale currency intervention by central banks would be required. And they would become increasingly reluctant to undertake such a task. In 1987 massive foreign central bank intervention was required to finance the U.S. current account deficit and prevent a collapse of the dollar. At the time, the intervention was largely, but not entirely, "sterilized"—that is, it did not lead to a big increase in domestic money supply in the countries that undertook the intervention. Sterilization, however, would become difficult if dollar reserves become a very large portion of the total assets of foreign central banks. Central banks took advantage of the dollar's strength in the spring and summer of 1988 to sell that currency. But if they again have to intervene massively to buy dollars due to a failure of private investors to do so, or to offset large net sales of U.S. securities by private foreign investors, they may be unable to avoid severe domestic monetary disruptions.

Foreign private investors and central banks together are more likely to be willing to finance *modest and declining* U.S. current account deficits for the next several years. In so doing they would avoid a sharp reduction in their own countries' net exports, and permit adjustment to take place without major disruption of domestic economies.

A reasonable *medium-term goal* is to cut the U.S. trade deficit by an annual *average* of 20–25 percent (roughly $35 billion in 1988) of its 1987 level over five years, with the aim of eliminating it completely by the end of 1992. That would, as noted, leave the United States with roughly a $60 billion current account deficit in 1992—about 0.75 percent to 1 percent of GNP in that year compared with a current account deficit of about 3.5 percent of GNP in 1987. With a large portion of the adjustment having taken place by that time, a new set of targets could then be set, aimed at bringing the United States into a trade surplus over the next four years. These targets will be difficult, but not impossible, to achieve. And even if not completely met, they can at least help establish the *direction* in which policies and markets need to move; they do not imply that governments should attempt to achieve them by fiat or make wrenching policy changes with other adverse implications. Nor should attaining these goals necessarily disrupt the international trading and financial system. The targets could be reached if some combination of the following occurs:

- The U.S. structural budget deficit falls by roughly $30–35 billion per year on average from its 1987 level;

• Domestic demand in the United States grows at an annual rate of roughly 1 percent *less* than the growth of output (GNP), with the difference going to increase net U.S. exports; domestic demand in Western Europe grows at an annual rate of 1–2 percent *higher* than in the United States, and by about 1 percent *higher* than European output, with the difference resulting in increased net imports; and domestic demand in Japan grows by 2–3 percent *higher* than in the United States, and at a rate of about 1 percent *higher* than Japanese GNP, again with the difference resulting in increased net imports. In 1987, U.S. domestic demand grew by 2.5 percent, while output grew by 3.0 percent. In contrast domestic demand grew by roughly 5 percent in Japan, while output rose by 4.2 percent. And domestic demand rose by 3.7 percent in Organization for Economic Cooperation and Development (OECD) Europe, while output increased by 2.5 percent. So the differentials suggested here as targets do not require enormous changes in output/domestic demand relationships compared with those recently established;
• Imports of OPEC countries grow by 3 percent per year in volume, up from current rates, but about one-half their rate in the boom years from 1969 to 1978;
• Latin American imports from the U.S. grow by about 10 percent annually (below the 16 percent growth in the boom years of 1975–81, but well above the –6 percent figure recorded from 1981–86);
• East Asian NIC imports from the United States grow at 2–3 percent above recent rates, which have been about 25 percent per year on average;
• The United States regains global market share lost during the period of dollar overvaluation. In the 1975–80 period U.S. exports accounted for between 11.5 percent and 13 percent of world trade; by 1986 they had fallen to 10.7 percent;
• Foreign direct investment in the United States continues to grow by about $35–40 billion per year, with increasing emphasis on the building of new plants, thus leading non-American companies to supply more of the U.S. market from U.S.-based factories, rather than from abroad, and creating new jobs in the United States;
• U.S. gross savings increase from their 1987 level of 12.6 percent of GNP to roughly 16 percent (the 1949–81 average) while gross private domestic investment grows to roughly 17 percent of GNP, one percentage point above its 1987 level and about the same amount above its 1949–81 average;
• The United States holds oil imports to below 45 percent of domestic consumption (they are now above 40 percent, and rising).

These are merely *rough approximations* of the size and types of developments that could lead to elimination of the U.S. trade deficit and a significant reduction of the U.S. current account deficit by the end of 1992. Less important than the precise order of magnitude is the general set of developments indicated by these figures. A combination of these targets needs to be realized. Some will occur due to market forces, such as trade and investment shifts induced by currency movements; but they cannot happen without supportive government policies, for example, a reduction in the U.S. budget deficit to increase savings and free up resources both for new investment and for additional exports, greater American emphasis on education, stimulus (plus structural change) abroad to ensure rising domestic demand overseas, and a more purposeful global effort to reduce debt-imposed constraints on Third World growth.

International Considerations: A Comprehensive Strategy

The policy instruments that can reduce the U.S. current account deficit are largely economic. But politics govern the use of these instruments, and they are strongly affected by social conditions and historical traditions in individual countries. The Group of Seven has strengthened the process of policy harmonization and has, to a degree, "guided" currency markets at critical moments. But the goal of achieving *domestic* policy changes capable of producing a sustained decline in trade and current account imbalances has proved elusive.

Even when ministers and officials have agreed on broad objectives, they have often found themselves in disagreement on appropriate policies for achieving those objectives. For example, in West Germany there is negative population growth, an aversion to trade deficits, and an even greater aversion to inflation—due to memories of the economic and political disasters of the 1920s and 1930s; governments there since the war have avoided policies that risk inflation. Moreover, the highly developed domestic infrastructure limits the number of projects that the government could finance even if it wanted to stimulate growth through additional spending. The Germans are skeptical, indeed often fearful, of stimulative policy prescriptions from Washington, where institutional memories are not about inflation but of the Great Depression; the United States thus tends to make unemployment the primary economic enemy, leading American government officials to resort more easily to stimulative policies.

Questions such as how much countries in trade surplus should adjust (for example, how far they should allow their currencies to appreciate, or how much they should stimulate their economies, in order to help deficit countries to move toward trade balance), and how much responsibility deficit nations must accept for reducing their imbalances, have plagued the international monetary and trading systems for years.

The world economy is organized today on the basis of integrated international financial and goods markets. So sharply divergent national policy approaches often lead to currency or financial volatility and ultimately imperil global economic stability. An international strategy for better-balanced and sustained growth in the world economy is a growing necessity, as opposed to efforts by nations to avoid adjustment or shift the burden to others. Nor can nations with impunity insulate certain sectors from global competition when it suits their needs while supporting openness in the areas in which their industries do well.

Lofty global goals, however, do not normally carry much political weight with national leaders. Leaders tend to evaluate carefully the costs and benefits of proposals for policy change, or policy "concessions," put forward by other nations in the name of global growth or equilibrium, in order to determine whether these serve their immediate interests and to be sure their nations do not give up more than others, or obtain too few advantages. So improvements that benefit the global economy but do not appeal to proximate national interests are likely to fall on deaf ears.

Given this environment, two political realities must govern the adjustment process:

- The United States cannot blame its trade deficit entirely, or even largely, on others or expect them to make policy changes that solve those problems that are primarily the result of U.S. domestic policy. If this country takes measures that are in its own self-interest, such as reducing its budget deficit in a responsible way, and if it confronts underlying problems such as low savings and high consumption, then it will be in a stronger position to ask other countries to contribute more vigorously to the global adjustment process. If it turns inward, protects its market, threatens unilateral troop withdrawals, or fails to "put its own house in order," it will impair its credibility and weaken its global political leadership. In a similar spirit the United States must accept the reality that, in an era of more broadly shared economic power, it can no longer dominate the international economic fora to the extent it did in earlier years; today its approach to international economic leadership cannot be based, as in the past, on the assumption that its economic partners will support its position in deference to America's power. Instead it must lead by example and by building coalitions in economic summits, the Group of Seven, the General Agreement on Tariffs and Trade (GATT), or the International Monetary Fund (IMF).

- The preferred political *and* economic solution to the U.S. external debt problem is one that fosters higher world growth with price stability, and thus emphasizes a sustained expansion of U.S. exports, coupled with import substitution, rather than one based on contracting imports sharply through protectionism or recession. Given the high unemployment in many countries, overleveraging in the U.S. economy, and a still-serious Third World debt problem, a contractionary approach risks a world slowdown and financial turbulence. But a successful export expansion strategy depends on a willingness *abroad* to achieve sustained and strong domestic demand and accept rising imports; America's trading partners must, in this connection, resist pressures from their industries for protection or subsidies to offset large trade corrections vis-a-vis the United States. Without this positive set of reinforcing actions abroad, trade balance can only come through abruptly declining U.S. imports.

Whatever the pace of adjustment, it is the surpluses of Japan, Western Europe (particularly West Germany), and a number of major NICs that will inevitably have to decline the most as the United States reduces its trade deficit.

With respect to Japan, the first Maekawa report, commissioned by former prime minister Nakasone to recommend how that country should respond "to the recent environmental changes surrounding Japan in the international economic situation," stressed the "goal of steadily reducing the nation's current account imbalance to one consistent with international harmony."[2] Achieving that goal will probably require the country to be in trade equilibrium with the rest of the world sometime in the first half of the next decade. Even so, Japan's net external asset position—which will approach $700 million in the early 1990s—would earn it interest and dividends abroad sufficient to run large current account surpluses.

Western Europe collectively, and West Germany in particular, will likewise see a significant reduction in its trade surplus with the rest of the world, as will the newly industrializing countries of East Asia. Canada, America's largest trading partner, will probably realize a reduction in its trade surplus; although because it already has a current account deficit, its overall contribution to the adjustment will be relatively small. Latin America's trade balance with the United States will also weaken, but only if it can obtain additional financing on reasonable terms and can sell more of its products in Europe and Asia.

The contributions of individual nations to better equilibrium cannot, of course, be measured only in terms of their bilateral balances with the United States. Thus Japan and West Germany—as well as the smaller countries of East Asia—can foster a better global balance vis-a-vis the United States not only by directly reducing trade surpluses with the United States, but also by "triangulation," that is, by importing more goods from other nations, thus enabling them to buy more from the United States. For instance, Japan, Western Europe, and the NICs of East Asia are large importers of commodities. If Latin American nations were to enjoy a spurt in commodity exports to those countries, they could in turn buy more American products.

The following measures, discussed in detail below, could promote movement toward equilibrium between the United States and its trading partners:

I. Pursuit of mutually consistent domestic economic adjustment policies by the United States and its major trading partners, predicated on the notion that domestic demand should rise more rapidly abroad than in the United States for the next several years;
II. Additional moderate changes in exchange rates, coupled with an effort to reduce currency volatility in order to stabilize the global trade and investment environment;
III. Reduced constraints on Latin American growth;
IV. Increased U.S. industrial capacity and productivity; and
V. The maintenance and improvement of a liberal international trade and investment system.

Let us address each of these in order.

I. *Substantial changes in the rate of growth of domestic demand relative to domestic production in the United States and in its trading partners will be important to achieving a smooth reduction in America's trade deficits.* To eliminate the U.S. trade deficit by the end of 1992, as noted above, production of tradable goods and services must expand by about $170 billion relative to consumption of these items. That is, the United States should be consuming annually about 1 percent less than its yearly gains in production and exporting 1 percent more; its trading partners together would need to consume more than they produce in order to absorb the increase in U.S. exports. In the case of the United States, increased productive capacity, coupled with a slowing in the rate of growth of domestic consumption in favor of additional savings, will be required for the economy to meet growing export demand without placing enormous strains on existing capacity, and in so doing creating intense inflationary pressures. To the extent that more capacity is built, the requirement for a slowing of domestic consumption is lessened somewhat. But slower growth in consumption must still make a contribution to the process; it is needed to shift a greater portion of income into savings in order to narrow the savings-investment gap. The key here is to strike the right balance. If all of the trade improvement is the result of a decline in domestic consumption—that is, if consumption fell by enough to reduce net imports by the full $170 billion, the result would be a recession or a depression in the United States. So lower consumption can bear only part of the burden. The larger portion must be borne by import substitution and by increasing exports, and to do so without creating inflation means adding new productive capacity.

The entire economy will have to adjust to bring about a situation in which production exceeds consumption by an amount sufficient to eliminate the trade deficit. But, as the 1988 Economic Report of the President pointed out, "The *structural* adjustments required to reduce the U.S. trade deficit are relatively larger than the *macroeconomic* adjustments."[3] This is because tradable goods and services account for only 40 percent of *overall* U.S. GNP. By definition nontradable goods cannot be exported or substituted for imports. So the 40 percent of the economy that produces tradable goods and services must bear the *entire burden* for the trade correction. To reduce the trade deficit by nearly 4 percent of GNP, that is, to eliminate it, production of tradable goods and services must expand by *9-10 percent* relative to consumption of this category of items. Unless consumption of tradable items actually declines, as opposed to rising more slowly, the production of tradable goods and services will have to expand by *well over* 9-10 percent during the next few years. If, for example, consumption of these goods grows at the 1988 rate of over 2.5 percent in each of the next four years, production will need to grow by a total of over 20 percent during that period. In 1987, according to the President's Council of Economic Advisers, production of tradable goods grew at about a 5 percent rate. It is questionable whether that rate can be sustained for several years, much less increase, without severe price pressures in major sectors of the economy, unless new capacity is brought on-stream.

The United States has cut the federal budget deficit from its recent highs. This has contributed to slower domestic demand and freed up savings to meet additional private investment requirements. But without further spending cuts and revenue increases, the deficit—and therefore government dissaving—is likely to remain high for the next several years. And should economic growth weaken, the deficit would rise substantially.

The optimum pace for cutting the budget deficit is somewhat greater than that for cutting the current account deficit. If the budget deficit were to fall more slowly than the current account deficit (looked at another way, the current account deficit represents the total import of capital), the government would be absorbing a larger portion of a smaller aggregate capital pool. It would therefore be crowding out private investment. Thus the goal should be to reduce the structural budget deficit by about $30-35 billion per year for the next few years.

There are, of course, many possible approaches to reducing the U.S. budget deficit. Whatever is done will require an economic-political compromise, including civilian and military spending curbs with some tax increases. The 1987 postcrash budget compromise—while helpful in avoiding an increase in the deficit that would have occurred without this pact—postponed a number of the tough choices required to produce eventual elimination of the structural deficit, that is, place the budget on a trajectory that would enable it eventually to reach a balance under conditions of full employment. To do so, a bolder agreement must be forged between major political constituencies.

Because a number of programs have been substantially reduced in recent years, new opportunities for cuts are going to be difficult to find. Moreover, although the public wants expenditure cuts, it also wants substantial government services. For example, in November 1987, 59 percent of those responding to an NBC-*Wall Street Journal* poll said that they did not care enough about the budget deficit to pay higher taxes.[4] Other polls indicate that large constituencies want the government to spend more on stopping crime, improving education, increasing housing for the homeless, strengthening the health-care system, and bettering the environment. Nonetheless, spending cuts must be part of the compromise, probably accounting for the major share of the deficit reduction. One promising idea, suggested to the president by a group of Republican senators in 1985, is to put a "cap" on certain cost-of-living adjustments (COLAs) in retirement programs. The president rejected this. But reducing some non–poverty related COLAs—that is, COLAs for upper-income individuals—could significantly reduce expenditures. There could be full indexing of COLAs to inflation for individuals in lower-income groups, and only partial, or zero, indexing for those in upper-income groups. A similar effect could be achieved without a "means test," which many people find distasteful, through use of the tax system; that is, a portion or all of such benefits could be taxed like ordinary income for individuals in upper-income brackets.

The overall process for deciding on spending cuts should be based on a zero-based budgeting exercise. The president would insist on an audit of each program to determine its relative merits, priority, and efficiency in meeting its goals; that exercise would help him determine how much money each program should receive relative to others. It would lead to reduction or elimination of funding for programs that were instituted or expanded in an earlier era, in which resources were in greater abundance, but can no longer pass the test of need or efficiency.

Limits on the growth of military spending must be part of the package, in part because increased efficiencies are available there, in part because this spending category accounts for a large portion of the budget, and in part because a politically acceptable package, including cuts in social and other domestic programs, cannot be forged without limits on military expenditures. Washington should also consider a two-year military budget cycle to improve planning and efficiency.

Slowing the growth of America's military budget should not be carried out by simply slicing the funds of each military service equally, but should be based on an overall strategic plan. Putting that together will require a fundamental reexamination of how this nation can continue to play a strong global security role, and be fully prepared to meet all likely risks to its security interests, with greater efficiency. That will require a reassessment of the missions of the various services and the most efficient way of meeting them, along with a greater contribution to Western, particularly European, defense by America's allies. The new president can take an important initiative by calling for a NATO high-level "wise men" group, including military as well as economic experts. This group should be mandated to recommend a strategy for Western, particularly European, security for the remainder of this century, to determine how most efficiently to permit NATO to respond to potential threats and to strike a better balance between the contributions of Western nations to the common defense and their available resources. Achieving greater efficiency will also require a more rigorous effort by the four military services in the United States, and by the NATO allies together, to reduce the duplication of weapons systems.

Tax increases, like most program cuts, are unpopular. But to the degree they are needed to permit significant cuts in the deficit and permit the nation to fund programs needed to meet domestic requirements neglected in recent years—such as low-income housing and education—and essential defense needs, and they probably are, one promising approach would be to expand the use of sales or excise taxes. A tax on consumption (as opposed to an investment-inhibiting tax such as an increase in the capital gains tax) could raise revenue, slow the growth of domestic demand, and boost savings without slowing the pace of investment in new plant and equipment. It could be narrowly based (that is, on only a few items) or broadly based. Regressivity should be avoided by exempting food, clothing, and medicine. This approach to taxes, coupled with a lower rate of growth in defense spending and upper-income COLA caps, could provide the basis for a consensus on deficit reductions. It is important, however, to keep the tax portion of this equation relatively low. America has a savings deficit as well as a budget deficit; reducing the budget deficit at the expense of private savings by enacting a sizable tax increase would not reduce the nation's dependence on imported capital and would thus block the improvement of our current account position.

Growth abroad needs to be vigorous to complement domestic adjustment in the United States. The OECD projects growth in domestic demand in Japan at 5.5 percent in 1988 but predicts that it will taper down to a still healthy 4.25 percent in 1989. It predicts that Europe will attain growth of 3.25 percent in 1988 (which it will probably exceed) and 2.25 percent in 1989. The OECD also foresees the U.S. current account deficit declining only marginally—to $150 billion in 1988 and $132 billion in 1989. Part of the higher growth in real demand in other OECD nations in 1987, it points out, came from lower import prices resulting from their stronger currencies and the fall in oil prices; these price declines added to domestic purchasing power, and that in turn spiked higher demand.[5]

In the early part of this decade, the fiscal policies of Europe and Japan were contractionary, while that of the United States was expansionary. That combination helped Japan and Europe enjoy export-led growth. Now the lower dollar and a weakening of net export volumes abroad have induced policy changes in these countries. Japan's robust domestic demand, induced by stimulative fiscal policy, including large government expenditures on public works and a tax cut, led to a 10 percent increase in import volume in fiscal 1987, with imports of manufactured goods accounting for a large portion of this increase. These changes have helped strengthen U.S. exports. But it will take a continued acceleration of net imports to effect substantial further improvements.

Japan is seeking to maintain its currently strong domestic demand. It has recognized that this is needed to reduce its trade surplus further and to help its industries to diminish their dependence on exports. But it also wants to avoid overheating its economy. Tokyo has set a goal of reducing its budget deficit, due to concerns about its high national debt and the enormous additional budgetary costs of social security in future years as its population ages. It is also undertaking a major tax reform to increase across-the-board sales taxes and eliminate excise taxes on sugar, gas, electricity, etc. In addition, Tokyo also plans to cut taxes on income, inheritance, and corporations. This package will inject, on the whole, a mild additional stimulus into the economy. The income tax cuts are also important to obtain popular support for other aspects of tax reform.

Tokyo is trying to moderate inflationary pressures by channeling more savings into infrastructure investment in order to reduce transportation bottlenecks and to increase economic activity in areas where cost pressures are less than in Tokyo. Monetary policy has been relatively restrained in light of inflationary concerns—which will be augmented as higher sales taxes raise prices.

For the foreseeable future Japan will have a tough balancing act. It will need to sustain an expansion of domestic demand sufficient to steadily reduce its trade and current account surpluses, while exercising care that it does not allow excessive price pressures to emerge in the economy.

Turning to Europe "forward-looking indicators point to continued strength," but in the region's major economy expectations of a future decline in demand are discouraging further capital formation.[6]

The Commission of the European Community, in July 1987, urged Bonn to agree to early implementation of planned tax cuts and advancement of incentives for infrastructure investment.[7] Since that time, West Germany's five leading economic research institutes have expressed the fear—so far proved exaggerated—that growth in 1988 would be modest due in part to planned increases in consumption taxes.

More broadly, the Commission's report suggested the need for limited and temporary budgetary stimulus in a number of major European nations, and called for a Europe-wide effort to boost growth in light of the close economic linkage among members of the Community. But the importance of the West German economy to the rest of Europe implies a relatively greater role for that nation in any European growth scenario. Much of the rest of Europe has large trade deficits with West Germany. Because of such deficits, other European nations are reluctant to stimulate domestic growth for fear of a further erosion of their trade balances.

Bonn is providing financial assistance to poorer areas of Europe—a Euro-stimulus policy—which should be encouraged and expanded. But German growth itself remains central to that in the rest of Europe. If West Germany expands its economy, and in doing so boosts imports from its European neighbors, they in turn can stimulate growth without fearing a large deterioration of their trade balances. Most do not wish to invite a further weakening of their exports by stimulating before, or growing for very long at a higher rate than, the Germans.

But German growth cannot be achieved using the same techniques as Japan, in part because West Germany does not have the backlog of unmet economic infrastructural needs that Japan has (that is, its roads, housing, and hospitals are more modern than those in Japan). Bonn has decided to reduce subsidies significantly in 1989, which should increase the efficiency of resource allocation. But more ambitious programs to improve the flexibility of labor markets, deregulate markets for goods and services, and cut social security taxes on employment would strengthen prospects for increased growth and for a decline in the nation's stubbornly high rate of unemployment. And an increase in depreciation allowances could substantially boost investment. There is another group of countries in Europe, for example, Holland and Switzerland, whose situation is similar to that of West Germany. In these cases structural measures are also warranted in order to boost domestic demand without increasing inflation.

Britain, France, and Italy, face constraints on their growth resulting from trade deficits. Because their currencies are linked (in Britain's case, implicitly) in the European Monetary System (EMS) to the deutschemark, devaluations needed to improve their competitiveness have not taken place. Considerable benefits might be gained by managing the EMS—which has been so successful in arresting inflation—in such a fashion that trade deficit countries are allowed greater latitude to lower their exchange rates for a time. While price stability, an important goal of the EMS, should remain a high priority, such a shift in currency relationships could give trade deficit countries an opportunity to increase domestic demand a notch or two without suffering a deterioration in their trade positions.

Structural problems must also be dealt with on a European-wide basis. In most of Western Europe, growth and employment would be given a boost by measures aimed at reducing subsidies and rigidities in goods and labor markets. Success in creating a "single European market" without internal barriers to the movement of goods, services, people, or money—and without extensive disparities in internal regulations—would improve efficiency to a significant degree and spur noninflationary growth. As it moves toward completion by the end of 1992, the single market should also attract new investment and expand trade with nonmember countries (so long as new impediments to imports are not imposed). A more unified market should also encourage Europe to stimulate demand through Europe-wide institutions such as the European Development Fund and the European Investment Bank; use of such institutions would diminish the inflationary and budgetary impact of stimulus in any one country, and could focus resources on projects with a high return in areas where capital cannot be raised by a single nation. By utilizing the borrowing authority of these institutions, Europe can mobilize capital without stretching government budgets. In addition, Europe-wide reductions in restrictions that make it difficult for employers to lay off workers could encourage more hiring, as could cuts in payroll taxes, which at current high levels constitute a disincentive to job creation (they raise costs to business without raising take-home pay for workers).

Robust domestic demand in other important OECD countries such as Canada and Australia must also play a role in reducing the U.S. current account and trade deficits. Both have made progress in reducing their fiscal deficits, and large new stimulus programs are not appropriate at the moment. But in both there is room for structural adjustment and increased private investment. In Canada, energy projects in Ontario and Quebec will strengthen domestic economic growth and demand for capital goods imports; structural improvements will also be driven by the government tax reforms.

The most compelling argument for additional stimulus in America's industrialized trading partners is their own self-interest. The massive shift in trade flows required to produce an improved global trade balance over the next five years will entail a loss of jobs and income in export-oriented, and import-sensitive, industries in Japan, Europe, and other nations *unless* they offset it by stronger domestic demand and structural improvements.

II. *Exchange rate adjustments must play a major role in promoting a reduction in global trade imbalances.* Much of the necessary adjustment of currencies has already occurred. But even with these adjustments and the changes in domestic economic policies discussed above, the further appreciation of a number of currencies vis-a-vis the dollar will probably be necessary over time.

The "proper" dollar exchange rate, one that will produce *significant and sustained* progress toward a current account balance, is not a theoretical calculation. It is rather a function of the outlook for domestic demand in the United States relative to that in its major trading partners, the magnitude of the present U.S. current account and trade deficits, the size of U.S. external debt, the level of interest and dividend payments on net foreign investment in the United States, and the attitudes of importers, exporters, and potential investors in new plant and equipment. If, for example, growth in domestic demand abroad were to accelerate significantly vis-a-vis that in the United States, and the rate of reduction in the U.S. trade deficit of mid-1988 were to continue, there would be little need for exchange rate adjustments. If, however, the progress in lowering the U.S. trade deficit slackens, and relative growth rate changes do not do more of the adjustment job, then the dollar's exchange rate will bear a very large share of the burden for achieving a reduction in the U.S. trade deficit.

For the exchange rate to promote current account equilibrium, assuming that is the ultimate goal, the dollar must fall *first* to the point at which U.S. goods *can* in theory be competitive on price grounds with foreign goods. By December 1987 that level had already been exceeded by a substantial amount vis-a-vis major currencies. But whether any given currency rate will produce significant and sustained trade improvements will depend on hard commercial decisions; for example, at what level does the dollar induce marginal foreign exporters to the United States, to decide to raise prices enough to cause loss of market share; at what level does it persuade American consumers to give up foreign goods to which they have become accustomed and switch to American-made goods; and at what level does it induce American companies to build new plant and put new equipment in operation at home geared to increasing exports and to invest time, management talent, and money in building up foreign marketing systems? And then there is the question, which will be addressed later, of how long the dollar will stay at competitive levels—and can governments overcome concerns of business that the currency will rise again, turning their investment and trade decisions sour.

Based on the exchange rates as of mid-1988, existing patterns of sourcing and investment, and expected inflation differentials among the major economies, most economists have predicted that the progress in lowering U.S. trade and current account deficits made in mid-1988 cannot be sustained. If that is the case, a lower dollar is inevitable. If there is strong evidence that the dollar must fall further to induce commercial decisions needed to further reduce the U.S. trade deficit, and markets begin to push it down, financial authorities should allow the adjustment to take place. Were they to try to hold the dollar at too high a level, to reduce inflationary pressures in the United States, in so doing slowing or reversing progress in reducing the U.S. trade deficit, the exchange rate will have little credibility. Investors in financial assets would likely insist on a risk premium for holding more dollar securities, and, as noted earlier in the chapter, that would drive up U.S. interest rates.

It is also true, of course, that a further fall in the dollar could raise U.S. interest rates, but here the analysis becomes more complex. After a fall in the dollar, interest rates are likely to rise, because that fall will increase prices. But that would be only a one-time increase, and it is an inevitable part of the trade adjustment process. It should not be of major concern to the Federal Reserve; the Fed's objective should not be to prevent the fall from occurring, but to avoid these one-time price increases from becoming incorporated into wages and leading to secondary price increases.

However, a drop of the dollar from a level deemed by investors to be too high will *also* reduce or eliminate the risk to foreign investors that they will suffer *currency losses* from holding dollar assets. That is, *after* the dollar falls to levels not deemed by the market to be artificially high, the currency risk is less. To the extent that investors had previously sought high interest rates to compensate them for the perceived currency risk, the dollar fall will exert *downward* pressure on interest rates. So there is a trade-off. A decline in the dollar from artificial heights will for one set off reasons (less currency risk) lead to downward pressure on interest rates; for another set of reasons (a higher level of inflation) it will increase rates. But if one has concluded that prolonged U.S. trade and current account deficits are not sustainable, and the dollar is too high, then allowing the dollar to decline in an orderly fashion, taking the one-time boost in inflation, in these circumstances is appropriate.

Although the dollar's relationship to the currencies of the major OECD countries—particularly Japan and West Germany—is the most critical, and has in recent years undergone the largest adjustment, the currencies of the newly industrialized areas of East Asia have become increasingly significant, and they must also make a contribution to international currency correction. Most European countries have permitted their exchange rates to appreciate at a rate similar to that of the deutschemark. But those of the East Asian exporters have lagged considerably behind the major currency of East Asia—the yen. That lag has helped producers in those countries to pick up a share in the U.S. market at the expense of countries, such as Japan, whose currencies have appreciated significantly. It has thus diluted some of the trade benefits expected by the United States from the dollar's decline against OECD countries.

By their very competitiveness, the developing nations of East Asia have earned a stronger position in world markets; but it would be appropriate for their currencies to continue to rise in value. These currencies need not appreciate to the same degree as the yen, because they did not decline as much as the yen in the early 1980s; however, a further rise for most is probably in order. The degree of adjustment is different for each of these currencies. Hong Kong and Singapore have current account positions that are relatively in balance, while Taiwan last year had a surplus of over $20 billion and Korea a surplus of over $10 billion. Foreign exchange reserves and external debt positions also differ considerably.

Europe and Japan, because their currencies have risen significantly vis-a-vis the dollar and most developing-nation currencies, should be expected in the future to import relatively more goods from developing nations, and the United States relatively less. Japan, in particular, should be in a position to absorb far more goods from East Asia; and indeed its imports from the region have surged over the past year. And currency adjustments of past years should induce both Europe and Japan to import more from Latin America. By taking a relatively greater share of developing-nation exports, Europe and Japan would deflect the nearly single-minded focus of East Asia and Latin America on the American market. (From 1981 to 1986 South Korean exports to the United States accounted for over 40 percent of that nation's economic growth; for Taiwan the figure was roughly 75 percent!) And because currency shifts have made many U.S. exports more competitive vis-a-vis those of Japan and Europe in the developing nations, U.S. exports should be able to pick up market share in those areas. Washington should insist that Europe and Japan avoid imposing artificial measures, such as government subsidies or tied aid, to prevent that market shift.

The East Asian countries need to take other actions to bring their current account surpluses down to more sustainable levels. Raising their exchange rates is important. But this must be part of a broader set of policies to reduce their dependence on export-led growth. Those countries with high import barriers need to step up the process of reducing them. Existing trade restrictions are less and less defensible for big trade surplus countries whose growth depends heavily on the openness of foreign markets to their product. Moreover, sitting on large piles of dollars is unwise economic policy; developing countries could better utilize these funds at home to improve domestic infrastructure, medical care, social security, and the environment in order to foster future economic growth and social progress. Most of these countries no longer have major balance-of-payments constraints, and thus can afford to liberalize their internal economies and boost living standards in a fashion consistent with the progress already made in increasing their manufacturing output.

The dollar probably needs to fall further over time vis-a-vis a broad range of currencies to put the United States on a steady path toward trade equilibrium early in the next decade. It certainly must decline at least enough to ensure that American goods do not suffer a loss of international price competitiveness due to the high rate of inflation in this country compared with that in its major trading partners. But any descent must be gradual in order to avoid disruption of trade and financial markets. Therefore, while there is a need for flexibility in the way the Group of Seven is managing exchange rates, there is also a need for a contingency strategy—however remote the contingency—to cope with, or avert, an "overshooting" of the dollar on the down side. So far, the purveyors of the notion that there would inevitably be a "hard landing," or "collapse," of the dollar have been proved quite wrong. In large measure this is because they had failed to appreciate the size and diversity of the U.S. capital market. Even when foreign investors moved out of bonds, they did not necessarily withdraw from all U.S. assets. Many invested in land, bought companies, acquired buildings, or built up large portfolios of equities. Moreover, central banks skillfully cooperated to buffer sharp falls in the dollar. But should confidence in the dollar collapse for, say political reasons, or because of a string of disappointing trade figures, a bold stabilization strategy would be required, such as the "dollar defense" package of November 1978. That involved strict monetary and fiscal tightening, large-scale intervention in currency markets, and an issue of U.S. bonds denominated in foreign currencies.

On the more optimistic side, once trade imbalances do show evidence of a steady decline, there is an opportunity to move toward a more stable monetary system. If the past several years have taught us anything, it is that exchange rate volatility causes importers, exporters, and prospective investors to place relatively little confidence in the price signals that any given set of exchange rates provides. That in turn contributes to long lags in the making of business decisions based on those rates, and thus slows the adjustment process. In a volatile environment, some investors will hesitate to build new plants in a country that has experienced a decline in its exchange rate, even if for the moment that investment looks profitable, for fear that the currency will rise sharply and render that investment unprofitable. Similarly, producers in a country whose currency has risen sharply often hesitate to raise the prices of their exports to the country with the lower currency to the point that they lose market share in that country. They instead hold their export prices down at close to the same levels, even if that means they lose money for a time, hoping that the importing country's depreciated currency will bounce back in a few months, which will enable their goods to regain profitability. Exporters in the country whose currency has dropped will be cautious about embarking on a program to sell abroad (with all the initial effort that requires) because currency shifts could render unprofitable their investment of time, money, and management.

If governments can establish, and markets accept, a currency range, or "zone," that provides a reasonable chance of achieving substantial progress toward trade equilibrium, and appear genuinely committed to maintaining that range for a sustained period of time by exhibiting a willingness to adjust domestic policies to do so, investment and selling decisions by the private sector can be made with greater confidence. Decision lags will diminish, thereby adding further momentum to trade corrections.

Placing greater emphasis on currency stability will also shift attention to the *domestic policy changes* that are required to validate, and take advantage of, the incentives for the reallocation of trade flows and the redeployment of domestic investment. If, for example, a nation's currency declines and domestic demand remains robust, then the domestic producer has less of an incentive to take advantage of his lower currency because he enjoys a strong domestic market; and domestic prices and wages are likely to increase, raising the costs of production.

III. A strategy for improving the U.S. trade and payments balance must include, as an integral part, *a strategy for reducing constraints on growth in heavily indebted developing nations,* particularly in Latin America. The major debtor countries devote over one-quarter of their export earnings to paying interest on their external debt; that outflow slows their domestic growth and retards investment; it also reduces their ability to import equipment and goods. And much of the cost is borne by U.S. exporters.

The next U.S. administration needs to reassess America's approach to the debt problem and to development assistance in the Third World; in particular it must put into clearer focus the relationship between the debt problem, slow growth in the developing world, and its efforts to improve the U.S. trade balance. It needs to recognize the importance of the multilateral development institutions in mobilizing huge sums of money in world capital markets for lending to the Third World; in a period of U.S. budget austerity, those institutions raise capital for developing nations with very little direct financial support, and virtually no appropriated funds, from the United States. They are a critical factor in restoring growth in heavily indebted Third World nations.

The major capital-exporting countries could make a contribution to growth in Latin America by absorbing a greater percentage of that region's exports. And to the extent that Europe and Japan wish to avoid bearing the vast brunt of the trade adjustment burden directly vis-a-vis the United States, or through additional stimulus in domestic demand, they have an interest in stimulating increased growth in Latin America by financing investment projects on that continent in countries pursuing sound domestic economic policies. Capital-exporting nations should also be encouraged to provide loan guarantees, and similar incentives, to induce their banks and other financial institutions (recognizing that it is the private sector, and not the government, to which large surpluses have accrued in these countries) to channel private savings to productive uses in the Third World.

Japan has committed itself to increase significantly concessional assistance to poorer nations. Most Japanese aid is provided to its neighbors in Asia, where it has been particularly helpful to the Philippines. But Japan's economic and political interests are global and the distribution of its aid should reflect that. Increased aid would be a constructive contribution to the recycling of Japan's surpluses. In light of Japan's small contribution to Western security and the many reasons for Japan to continue to play a modest military role,* its foreign aid should be the primary

*Japan can and should play a greater role in monitoring, air and sea surveillance, and antisubmarine activities in defense of sea lanes up to 1,000 miles from Japan—and be prepared to support U.S. aircraft carriers and other vessels when they are needed to assist Japan in the region. But the United States should not encourage Japan to go beyond this or to raise its defense expenditures for other types of military objectives. To do so would create serious apprehension throughout Asia and in the long run be counter to America's interests.

vehicle for it to support global stability and democracy. It should aim at raising its foreign assistance from roughly .3 percent of GNP to over 1 percent. And government incentives, as described above, can be used to encourage Japanese private institutions to make untied loans in parallel to those of the World Bank, the regional banks, and perhaps the U.S. Export-Import Bank for projects in indebted nations.

Western governments need to be imaginative in developing new techniques to encourage banks to sell or swap their Third World loans at market-related discounts. As in the case of the Morgan Guaranty/Mexico plan whereby Mexico issued new bonds, backed up by U.S. Treasury zero-coupon bonds, to replace old debts, these schemes should aim to substitute higher-quality debt instruments for riskier ones. More flexible regulatory arrangements should also be employed to enable holders of debt to swap these for shares in productive new investments, or to allow lower interest payments for a time without a major short-term tax impact. These and other ideas should aim at helping to transfer LDC obligations into more liquid, negotiable instruments in order to broaden the holdings of such debt, provide incentives for debtors to embark on needed economic reforms, be compatible with the goal of early resumption of voluntary lending, and allow for reduction in the now large net outflow of resources from debtors to private, government, and international institutional creditors.

Washington and its allies must see the debt issue as a common problem requiring concerted action. Managing the debt problem should not be regarded as simply a question of a sleight of hand by accountants or an exercise in staying one step ahead of a crisis, but as an effort to restore healthy growth in, and ultimately voluntary lending to, debtors. That is an integral part of the global adjustment process. It is also an issue directly related to the common security because high unemployment and social instability in Latin America—or the coming to power of radical leaders who are now challenging governments in major countries in Latin America—resulting from debt-induced austerity could lead to major political friction with the United States and a collapse of recently established democracies.

IV. American *manufacturing capacity, productivity, and quality of output must continue to improve* for the United States to take full advantage of the dollar's decline and growth abroad.

Whether the United States can fill growing export orders without encountering capacity constraints will depend heavily on the rate of investment in new capacity. Here there is room for optimism. U.S. capital spending in the manufacturing sector is expected to grow by 9 percent in 1988. Moreover, the planned levels of capital spending are especially high in industries such as primary metals (up 60 percent), paper (up 60 percent), and chemicals (up 26 percent), where capacity utilization is around historic peaks.

U.S. industry will have to continue to add considerable amounts of new capacity over the next few years to meet export demand without supply constraints. As stated above, to increase net exports by an amount equivalent to roughly 4 percent of GNP (that is, roughly $170 billion in 1987 dollars), the output of manufactured and other tradable goods (plus tradable services) must be raised significantly in order to fill increased export orders and meet new orders at home as Americans shift a portion of their purchases from foreign to domestically produced goods.

Increased productivity must complement increased production capacity. Although productivity in the U.S. manufacturing sector has increased significantly in recent years, continued growth is required. Foreign competition is attempting to meet the challenge of a lower dollar, and improved American competitiveness, by cost cutting, intensified marketing efforts, and quality improvements of its own. Through marketing experience, learning-curve gains, improvements in quality, stronger distribution channels, and related factors, many foreign companies are more formidable competitors in world markets than they were five years ago. And if the United States succumbs to the temptation to permit a surge in wages and prices in the period ahead, the benefits of the lower dollar and past improvements in productivity will erode very quickly.

The need for greater emphasis on productivity, and indeed overall trade competitiveness, was illustrated last year by H. Robert Heller, a member of the Board of Governors of the Federal Reserve. German imports from Japan, he noted, have risen far more rapidly than those from the United States over the past two years. "In many ways," he explains, "this is surprising. After all, the Japanese yen has remained roughly stable versus the German mark, while the dollar has become less expensive. On a simple price basis, the American exporter should hold the advantage. But the Japanese make up for this by a carefully designed marketing strategy, much determination, and total commitment to quality. They just try harder. Their success validates the appropriateness of that strategy."[8]

Further strides in improving U.S. productivity can be realized by increasing the efficiency of material flows, updating quality control procedures, and constantly applying state-of-the-art techniques to the production process. These can achieve substantial increases in quality and efficiency, permit the production of a flexible range of products, and close the time lag between the discovery of a new product and its appearance on the market. Too often the attraction of shifting production abroad to low-currency nations has permitted industries to avoid a hard examination of the organization and flexibility of their production process at home. In some cases, significant improvements in these areas could have kept production on our shores. Moreover, relocating production in cheap-labor/cheap-currency countries has often been less beneficial than expected, because labor costs have risen rapidly in some of the nations to which the investment has gone; and as products and production procedures have been modernized, labor has become a decreasing percentage of the cost.

In addition, some overseas investment and, more significantly, sourcing of key components abroad have resulted in the loss of American control over the production learning curve to other nations, hastening their ascent to higher rungs on the technology ladder. It is important that U.S. industry not rely wholly on the lower dollar to boost competitiveness, but see it as one more incentive to continuously update technology and worker knowledge in the production process, to regain control over the production of vital components, particularly to try to produce at home high-technology goods they now import, and to help utilize new technology and organizational techniques to strengthen production at the lower end of the product range, where new procedures and technologies can offset higher domestic wages.

The weakness of the U.S. trade balance in recent years should be a sharp reminder that a far greater effort must be devoted to shoring up the structural underpinning of the U.S. economy. Large trade deficits should end America's era of innocence about world trade based on the notion that we could always fall back on our large domestic market. In one area in which America has excelled, technology, other nations have caught up with, and in some cases surpassed, this nation's lead. And in both Japan and West Germany non-defense research and development expenditures have been rising as a percentage of GNP faster than in the United States. Several measures have been suggested by the Business Roundtable to revitalize U.S. competitiveness and technological leadership, including closer links between business and education (such as corporate participation in high school and college curriculum development and course instruction); establishment of national science and technology centers to foster government, academic, and business cooperation; the requirement that competitive impact statements accompany major regulatory and legislative proposals; and ensuring that the tax structure does not impede savings or research, development, and investment expenditures.[9]

These should be included as part of a broader pro-industrial strategy to boost U.S. productivity and trade competitiveness.

Underlying such a strategy must be a major national effort to strengthen America's attitude toward education—at all levels. Virtually every new industrial process requires a higher level of sophistication than its predecessor. This country has been careless about the quality of education. Only 8 percent of this nation's colleges and universities now require foreign language training, as opposed to 34 percent fifteen years ago. One out of four ninth graders will not graduate from high school.[10] The National Commission on Excellence in Education's 1983 report cites one analyst's candid view: "For the first time in the history of our country, the educational skills of one generation will not surpass, will not equal, will not even approach, those of their parents."[11] In Japan, teachers, by law, are paid salaries higher than other highly paid civil servants and are accorded great status in the community. In most other nations, education is a high social priority. In the United States, regrettably, it has not been. Unless attitudes change, beginning with families and extending to whole communities and to political leaders, and unless Americans make a sustained national commitment of resources and political leadership to investment in education, including teachers' salaries and educational facilities, the United States will fall further behind in this vital area.

Another area in which the United States is in danger of falling behind, with profound implications for its trade position, is energy. In 1987 the cost of oil imports surged to roughly $50 billion—a sum that exceeded one-quarter of the U.S. trade deficit. That figure was more than 45 percent above the level of 1986. Imports from the Middle East rose from 17 percent of total imports to 22 percent. In the same period daily U.S. crude production fell by about one million barrels. Experts expect imports soon to rise above their peak of 47 percent of consumption in 1977, with some predicting an annual oil bill of $150-200 billion within the next ten years.[12] To head off an emerging crisis, a program of long-range planning and investment is required. Tough choices need to be made to better utilize coal and hydro power, adjust tax and regulatory policy, augment expenditures for research and development on both conservation and new production techniques (including ways to develop alternative energy), clarify the role of nuclear energy, and step up exploration for new oil and gas reserves. Because of the long lead times, critical choices must be made soon.

V. Progress toward *liberalizing international trade* is also a vital part of a strategy to promote a smooth shift in global trade balances. There is an enormous risk that, as America's trading partners see their trade surpluses with the United States declining significantly, they will face intense domestic pressures to slow or resist this adjustment. Companies abroad that suffer from a weakening of competitiveness vis-a-vis American companies are likely to petition their governments for subsidies or import protection to defend themselves. If their governments acquiesce, the process of correcting large bilateral trade imbalances would be slowed considerably. Even if such measures were not aimed at the United States but at the Third World, the United States would be harmed because Third World exports would then be forced on the United States. And wholesale resort to protectionism abroad would trigger a series of countermeasures in this nation. Actions and reactions, retaliation and counterretaliation, would disrupt world trade, investment, and growth.

To understand better why foreign protectionist pressures might emerge as trade corrections continue, it is useful first to recognize that Americans, who see their trade in dollar terms, have a different perception of changes in trade balances than foreigners, who see their trade in terms of their own currencies. From Japan's perspective, for example, from April 1987 to March 1988 its trade surplus (on a customs-clearance basis, measured in dollars) was roughly $75 billion. This was a decline of roughly 16 percent, or $14 billion, from the previous year's figure of $90 billion. But when measured in yen terms, Japan's trade surplus declined from 14.4 trillion yen to 10.6 trillion yen—a drop of 26 percent. That is the way Japan sees it.

On a company-by-company basis, the phenomenon is similar. Even if profits in dollar terms were to remain the same for a Japanese company, they are much lower when translated back into yen because of the dollar's three-year fall vis-a-vis the yen. Indeed, this profit decline is part of the inducement for Japanese exporters to raise prices in dollar terms, or pull back from the U.S. market because of lower profits—both of which are part of the trade adjustment process.

And the impact of lower export profits will be highly concentrated in the manufacturing sectors of America's trading partners. Just as U.S. trade improvement will be advantageous primarily to manufacturers and service exporters, so will the pain of adjustment hit primarily the manufacturing and exportable service industries of Asia, Canada, and

Western Europe. Many companies in these sectors abroad will find it difficult to switch sales from the American market to their domestic markets. A large number have invested a great deal in their sales capabilities in the United States; for example, at the end of 1985 roughly 60 percent of Japan's direct investment in the United States was in the wholesale sector, in order to boost its exports to the United States. Many companies in Japan, West Germany, Britain, Korea, and other nations will wish to obtain subsidies to enable them to avoid loss of share in the United States; and others, facing stronger American exports of manufactured goods, will seek protection to limit the encroachment of American products in their home markets. To avoid this, a political-level agreement among the Group of Seven nations must be reached on a reasonable trajectory for reducing the U.S. trade deficit. Without broad acceptance among America's trading partners that the deficit must decline significantly, on the rough magnitude of the annual decline appropriate over the next several years, and on which nations' surpluses will need to be reduced or eliminated to accommodate this, the risk is great that individual nations will resist adjustment by taking protectionist actions.

In the absence of such an agreement, and probably even with one, the United States will need strongly to resist bilaterally and multilaterally foreign temptations to provide subsidies and other forms of protection. The GATT must become involved, because protectionist actions abroad will have a multilateral impact. One country's actions against an American product will divert U.S. goods to other markets, giving other countries an argument for taking restrictive measures.

By the same token, the United States itself will need to strike the right balance between asserting its legitimate right to challenge foreign trade restrictions and distortions—which it needs to do and will in some circumstances be compelled to do under the new trade law—and going so far in this direction that it gives other nations a pretext for imposing new restrictive measures of their own in retaliation. It must be borne in mind that, however slowly, the forces of trade are shifting in America's direction. We are beginning to regain lost market share. This is not a time to give other nations a pretext for thwarting the adjustment process.

Fortunately, the Uruguay Round of trade negotiations is now well under way. The promise of positive results in cutting world trade barriers, modernizing the rules and dispute settlement mechanisms of the GATT, and developing new procedures to limit subsidies, reduce barriers to trade in services, protect intellectual property, and expand trading opportunities in farm products would further allay protectionist pressures. These negotiations will not produce short-term cures for all the world's trading problems, but progress would make it difficult for governments to justify unilateral restrictions and help them to resist protectionist demands. Financial markets will have a keen interest in the results, because a fragmentation of the global trading system is likely to disrupt currency and capital flows.

Investment practices must also be dealt with, either in the GATT or in another multilateral forum such as the OECD. There must inevitably be a big increase in foreign direct investment in the United States as long as this country runs large current account deficits. Yet America, which has so often lectured developing and developed nations alike on the virtues of foreign investment and remains a large investor abroad, is now experiencing a surge of public displeasure with, and often outright hostility to, direct investment from overseas. With no international institution to monitor government policies toward investment, or establish norms of behavior, governments around the world have felt free to set arbitrary rules for, or limit, foreign direct investment. International investment rules or understandings are required to reduce the disparities in national practices and quiet fears of irresponsible behavior by foreign investors. The United States can have a powerful influence on the development of these rules—and contribute to the improved domestic atmosphere for new direct investment.

With or without such rules, however, many Americans will continue to be concerned that foreign companies can purchase U.S. companies at "bargain basement" prices due to the low dollar. The takeover figure to date is not large. In 1987 under one-third of the $41 billion direct foreign investment in this country was in the form of mergers and acquisitions; most was new, or "greenfield" investment, or reinvestment in existing facilities. Nevertheless, the debate is likely to intensify over the next few years, particularly if Americans perceive that Japan—whose corporate resources dwarf those of other nations and thus are seen as particularly "threatening"—will make large-scale or hostile acquisitions. Complicating the problem further, other countries' restrictions on inward direct investment raise concerns here that firms in this country can be bought by companies abroad while their own domestic companies are protected.

To be sure, every nation has a right to prevent foreign takeovers that jeopardize national security; and the United States has done so in the past. But the line must be drawn between exercising that right and extending government power in a way that limits legitimate, productive, and market-related investment. Investment in the United States is part of the trade and financial adjustment process. As foreign companies invest in the United States, goods they make here will replace imports. Moreover, foreign investments have brought new management methods, new technology, and new marketing techniques. In addition, direct investment is a less volatile form of investment than foreign purchases of U.S. securities; however, it does imply a greater degree of foreign control over specific U.S. industries.

But a loss of "control" of some sort is virtually inevitable if a country, such as ours, has a low savings rate and high borrowing needs; the difference is made up by imported funds, and those funds give the overseas investor a measure of influence. If these funds are used to purchase companies, the owners have influence over those companies. But foreign holding of bonds, and other securities, implies another type of influence—over U.S. capital markets. In short, unless the United States can narrow its savings/investment gap, it will be subject to greater influence from overseas because it will remain heavily dependent on foreign money. The only question will be the form that influence may take—over capital markets, over companies, or, more than likely, over both. So far this influence has not been used in a fashion inimical to U.S. interests; and there is little reason to believe that foreign investors in the United States have motives that differ dramatically from those that guide American investors abroad. However, it is appropriate for the United States to expect, and insist, that foreign investment comply with standards of "good corporate citizenship" in terms of labor relations and other business practices, while over time shifting more research, development, and value added to the United States.

Foreign direct investment, in one sense, reduces America's debt-service burdens. Interest on bonds, or bank accounts, must be paid in good times and bad. If the United States is in recession, this outflow might impose a cost on the U.S. economy and financial system. But with direct investment there is no automatic requirement of a payment. Dividends are paid on the basis of the performance of the investment. If the company and economy do well, profits will be higher, and can be sent abroad without a heavy cost to the U.S. economy. If the U.S. economy is sluggish and the company does badly, there is no requirement to repatriate profits, so during that period the drain would be less.

Conclusion

A broadly shared international political consensus regarding the degree and pace of reduction of the U.S. trade deficit must be developed. For the United States, new investment in plants and equipment, slower growth in consumption, improvements in productivity, higher savings, and a smaller budget deficit are the critical factors. For the world economy as a whole, higher growth, structural adjustment, an effort to ensure market-oriented exchange rates, and steps to maintain an open trading system must assume a high priority.

America's trading partners will have to increase net imports and the United States will have to increase net exports substantially in the period ahead to slow and ultimately halt the accumulation of U.S. external debt. Without an international consensus that a trade adjustment in the range of $150 to $170 billion over the next several years is necessary, and some understanding as to how it should be effected, America's trading partners will try to avoid the adjustment burden or shift it to one another; each will try to maintain as much of its trade surplus as possible in the hopes that other nations will take more of the burden. In fact, most major countries will have to give up a large portion of their trade surpluses—however difficult that may be. Many companies in those countries will suffer sharp falls in their exports and greater import competition. If America's trade partners do not have the political will to accept that, if large numbers of companies succeed in obtaining their governments' support to avoid having to make adjustments to this reality, and if there is inadequate domestic demand in those nations to help their companies offset this net export decline, the adjustment will be painful and disruptive to the world economy and financial markets.

The United States and its trading partners have had to confront major economic problems since 1970. They have had to reduce demand for imported oil, to squelch rampant inflation, and to manage the developing-country debt problem. But the adjustments required to stop the potentially disruptive buildup of American external debt may well turn out to be greater than any of these because the magnitude of the problem is so great. Yet adjustments of the type described in this chapter are feasible, and the targets I have outlined can be achieved with a purposeful approach and political commitment by the major trading nations. This effort should not be seen as simply an exercise in promoting international harmony. It is of critical importance to the economic and financial outlook in virtually all nations. Failure to curtail the buildup of U.S. external debt in an orderly fashion is likely to lead to disruption in currency and capital markets and major distortion in domestic economies—along with incalculable political friction.

Coordinated adjustment, in the final analysis, must be the goal of political leaders in this country and abroad over the next several years. Unless they summon the will and the wisdom to reduce global imbalances through a commonly agreed set of policies, the problem will overwhelm them, harming Western and Third World economies and undermining vital Western political and security relationships.

Notes

Chapter 1

For general background material, see Dewey R. Davis, *Financial History of the United States* (New York: Longmans, Green and Company, 1931); Herbert Feis, *Europe the World's Banker, 1870–1914* (New Haven: Yale University Press, 1930); Robert Solomon, "The United States as Debtor in the 19th Century," International Economic Letter, vol. 3, no. 1, Washington, D.C., January 18, 1983; and Jeffrey G. Williamson, *American Growth and the Balance of Payments, 1820–1918* (Chapel Hill: University of North Carolina Press, 1964).

1. Cleona Lewis, *America's Stake in International Investments* (Washington, D.C.: Brookings Institution, 1938), pp. 19–21.
2. Richard B. Morris, ed., *Encyclopedia of American History* (New York: Harper & Row, 1965), p. 53.
3. Ibid., p. 537.
4. Lewis, *America's Stake in International Investments,* pp. 163–64.
5. Morris, *Encyclopedia of American History,* p. 539.

Chapter 2

For general background material, see "Toll of the Twin Deficits" (A Statement of the Research and Policy Committee of the Committee for Economic Development, New York, July 22, 1987); and Shafique Islam, "America's Foreign Debt: Is the Debt Crisis Moving North," *Stanford Journal of International Law* 23, no. 1 (1987).

1. U.S. Department of Commerce, *United States Trade Performance in 1987* (Washington, D.C.: Government Printing Office, June 1988), p. 130.
2. Charles K. Brown, "European Chemical Industry—1988 Prospects" (London: Goldman Sachs Research, February 22, 1988), p. 7.
3. Benjamin M. Friedman, "Increasing Indebtness and Financial Stability in the United States," Harvard University, Cambridge, Mass., July 1986, Table 1.
4. Paul A. Volcker, Testimony before the U.S. Congress, Joint Economic Committee, 99th Congress, February 2, 1987, p. 6.
5. Portions of this analysis of Japan are drawn from Kent E. Calder, Testimony before U.S. Congress, Joint Economic Committee, 99th Congress, December 11, 1986; and Jeremy Hale, "Japan: Macro-Economic Background for Financial Markets" (London: Goldman Sachs Research, May 28, 1987).

6. Portions of this analysis of West Germany are drawn from Gavyn Davies, "The German Growth Conundrum" (London: Goldman Sachs Research, January 22, 1987).

Chapter 3

For general background material, see Rudiger Dornbusch, "The Need for Further Dollar Depreciation" (Paper prepared for the conference on the exchange rate of the dollar, Washington, D.C., Institute for International Economics, June 1987); Robert D. Hormats, *Reforming the International Monetary System* (New York: Foreign Policy Association, June 1987); Shafique Islam, "The Dollar and the Policy-Performance-Confidence Mix," *Essays in International Finance,* no. 170 (Princeton University, July 1988); Paul Krugman, "Sustainability and the Decline of the Dollar," Brookings Discussion Papers in International Economics (Washington, D.C.: Brookings Institution, March 1987); and John Williamson, "The Dollar Is Near Its FEER" (Paper prepared for the conference on the exchange rate of the dollar, Washington, D.C., Institute for International Economics, July 1987).

1. For key aspects of this analysis I am indebted to David Morrison and Jeremy Hale, "The Search for Equilibrium Exchange Rates" (London: Goldman Sachs Research, February 16, 1987).

2. Martin Feldstein, "Correcting the Trade Deficit," *Foreign Affairs*, Spring 1987, p. 797.

3. *Economic Report of the President* (Washington, D.C.: Government Printing Office, February 1988), p. 77.

4. Hobart Rowen, "How Baker Talked the Dollar Down," *The Washington Post*, June 8, 1986, p. D1.

5. Karl Otto Poehl, "Are We Moving towards a More Stable International Monetary Order?" (Paper presented at the Centennial Conference of the International Herald Tribune, Paris, April 15, 1987), p. 10.

6. Hobart Rowen, "How Baker Talked the Dollar Down," *The Washington Post*, June 8, 1986, p. D1.

7. Ibid.

8. *World Economic Outlook, April 1987* (Washington, D.C.: International Monetary Fund), p. 9.

9. Charles K. Brown, "European Chemical Industry—1988 Prospects" (London: Goldman Sachs Research, February 22, 1988), p. 15.

10. Ibid.

11. Department of Commerce, *United States Trade: Performance in 1987* (Washington, D.C., 1988), p. vii.

12. Kenneth N. Gilpin, *International Herald Tribune*, July 28, 1987, p. 13.

13. "Toll of the Twin Deficits" (Statement of the Research and Policy Committee of the Committee for Economic Development, New York, July 22, 1987), p. 4.

14. Communique of the finance ministers and Central Bank governors of the Group of Seven, International Monetary Fund, Washington, D.C., February 22, 1987. (Italy did not participate in the final communique.)

15. David Morrison, "The Fundamental Pressures on the Dollar" (London: Goldman Sachs Research, May 12, 1987).

16. Martin Feldstein, "A Self-interested Way to Avoid Death in Venice," *Financial Times* London, May 20, 1987.

17. Rimmer de Vries, "It Has Declined, But Still Not Enough," *The New York Times*, January 11, 1987.

18. *World Economic Outlook, April 1987* (Washington, D.C.: International Monetary Fund), p. 18.

19. Statement of the Group of Seven, International Monetary Fund, Washington, D.C., December 22, 1987.

Chapter 4

1. *World Economic Outlook, April 1987* (Washington, D.C.: International Monetary Fund), p. 80.

2. Stephen Fay and Hugo Young, "The Day the L Nearly Died," monograph reprinted from Sunday *Times* of London, June 1978, p. 10.

3. Ibid., p. 21.

4. Ibid., p. 25.

Chapter 5

1. Paul A. Volcker, Testimony before the U.S. Congress, Senate, Committee on Banking, Housing, and Urban Affairs, 99th Congress, February 19, 1987 (Washington, D.C.: Government Printing Office, 1987).

2. Ibid., p. 27.

3. Ibid., pp. 24, 25.

4. Alan Greenspan, Statement before the U.S. Congressional Summit, New York, December 1986.

5. Martin Feldstein, "Correcting the Trade Deficit," *Foreign Affairs*, Spring 1987, p. 801.

6. Testimony of C. Fred Bergsten in U.S. Congress, Joint Economic Committee, 99th Congress, July 1, 1987 (Washington, D.C.: Government Printing Office, 1987), p. 8.

7. Peter G. Peterson, "The Morning After," *The Atlantic*, October 1987, p. 45.

8. Statistics drawn from reports of the Securities Industry Association, New York.

Chapter 6

For general background material, see C. Fred Bergsten, "Economic Imbalances and World Politics," *Foreign Affairs*, Spring 1987, pp. 770–94; Martin Feldstein, "Correcting the Trade Deficit," *Foreign Affairs*, Spring 1987, pp. 795–806;

and U.S. Congress, Joint Economic Committee, "The Economy at Midyear: A Legacy of Debt," August 5, 1987, Washington, D.C. (the source of the charts in this book).

1. *The Wall Street Journal*, March 17, 1988, p. 1.

2. Report of the Advisory Group on Economic and Structural Adjustment for International Harmony, Government of Japan, Tokyo, April 7, 1986, p. 2.

3. *Economic Report of the President* (Washington, D.C.: U.S. Government Printing Office, 1988).

4. *The Wall Street Journal*, November 30, 1987, p. 1.

5. *Economic Outlook* (Paris: Organization for Economic Cooperation and Development, June 1988), p. vi.

6. Bank for International Settlements *Annual Report 1988*, Basel, pp. 11–14.

7. Communique of the Commission of the European Communities, "The Economic Outlook for 1988 and Budgetary Policy of the Member States," Brussels, July 3, 1987, p. 35.

8. H. Robert Heller, "The International Challenge—How Will America Respond?" (Speech to the Federal Reserve Bank of Atlanta, February 12, 1987), p. 9.

9. The Business Roundtable, "American Excellence in a World Economy: A Summary of the Report," New York, June 15, 1987.

10. "Common Sense in Competitiveness," (Atlanta: The Carter Center, April 1988), p. 8.

11. Paul Copperman, Report of the National Commission on Excellence in Education, as cited in Robert D. Hormats, "The International Economic Challenge," *Foreign Policy*, no. 71, Summer 1988, p. 106.

12. U.S. Energy Association, "Countdown to the Next Crisis," Washington, D.C., April 1988, p. 1.

Index